The Potatopia Cookbook

The Potatopia Cookbook

77 Recipes Starring the Humble Potato

Allen Dikker

Photography by Melissa Hom

SURREY BOOKS

AN AGATE IMPRINT

CHICAGO

The Potatopia slogan was written by Shebang Studio.

Printed in China

The Potatopia Cookbook
ISBN 13: 978-1-57284-220-5
ISBN 10: 1-57284-220-2
ebook ISBN 13: 978-1-57284-798-9
ebook ISBN 10: 1-57284-798-0

First printing: January 2018

10 9 8 7 6 5 4 3 2 1   18 19 20 21 22

Surrey Books is an imprint of Agate Publishing. Agate books are available in bulk at discount prices. For more information, visit agatepublishing.com.

I dedicate this book to my wife, Galina, and my two boys, Landen and Kyle, for their support and vital taste-testing abilities and ideas. I love you dearly.

Our Potatopians

For you, and you, and you, and you,
and for you over there in line. We
have potatoes for the vegans and
the omnivores, for the foodies and
the families. We have fully loaded
potatoes for the hungry ones. We
have shoestrings, chips, and curly
cuts for the kids. And we have
cheese fries for the fanatics (and for
a few hungover friends). We have
signature suggestions for the first-
timers and a build-your-own bar for
the regulars. So come one, come all.
There are potatoes for everyone!

Contents

Introduction
The Story of Potatopia

GROWING UP IN BROOKLYN, I could often be found crunching away on a bag of garlic and onion potato chips at Jimmy's Famous Heros, a neighborhood sandwich shop. This was my heaven. As a kid, I couldn't have been more obsessed with the salty snack. Many of us were—and still are. But I had a true addiction to them. If not stopped, I could eat potato chips for breakfast, lunch, and dinner.

Little did I know as a kid that my future career and the birth of a new fast-casual concept restaurant would revolve around my favorite food—a simple tuber and the basis of all chips: the humble potato.

But it wasn't always about potatoes.

I was born in Brooklyn after my parents emigrated from Odessa, Ukraine, which had been ravaged by dictatorship, poverty, and violence in the 1970s. My parents were hardworking people with no college degrees. I was lucky to have not only their guidance, love, and support, but also that of my grandparents, who came with my parents to the United States and took care of my brother and me while my father worked two jobs, as a factory worker at a meat-processing plant and as a taxi driver at night. My mother spent her days working at a jewelry exchange in Manhattan. Eventually, my father took a leap and borrowed enough money to own his own taxi medallions. Later, he moved on to other ownership ventures: vending machines, car washes, gas stations, and eventually commercial properties. By the time I was 10 years old, we were able to afford a move to a larger home in Staten Island, and then on to Marlboro, New Jersey, when I was 14.

As you might have noticed, my parents' story embodies that age-old idea of the American Dream: making sacrifices, taking risks, and working hard to achieve success in work, in family, and in life. These messages helped guide me throughout my childhood, and to this day, my father's entrepreneurial spirit continues to inspire my own.

From a young age, my brother and I followed my father around as he built his various businesses. We would sit in meetings with him, follow his moves, and listen to his dealings. After my mother decided to leave her job to help my father, we also took note of how she handled all the administrative work needed for the businesses. I feel lucky—these experiences gave me some serious street smarts when it comes to running my own business, which is no easy task. I have always strived to work hard and honor my education, a luxury my parents did not have.

I was a good student, but my focus in my teens was primarily on tennis. I trained vigorously with a strict Russian coach who helped me earn high-ranking status as a junior tennis player, and some of my peers even went on to become pros. I didn't realize until later how much my tennis training had given me in terms of the discipline, stamina, focus, and drive not only to work hard at something but also to strive to be the best, even if it means working through the hardest of challenges. This sports mentality, coupled with my college degree in business and my parents' influences, steered me toward the world of entrepreneurship.

In 2004, I started my own media advertising company called Trivista Media Group. In my years with Trivista, I traveled nine months out of the year—most of it by myself. During my downtime, I became a classic foodie and sought out all the local flavors and the best restaurants. Around this time, I met Galina, who would not only become a wonderful wife and mother but also my "foodie in crime" and, very importantly, the ultimate food tester and partner in the kitchen.

When the recession hit in 2008, my media company suffered tremendously. During a recession, media and advertising are always the first things companies cut. When the Dow Jones fell to 6,000, I felt the hit instantly. For two years, I managed to keep the company afloat, but consumer confidence in my product dwindled as more budgets continued to get cut. Things were stressful. So stressful, in fact, that they actually drove me into the kitchen—not a place you would usually find me unless it was to eat. But I soon found an undeniable sense of relief and calmness cooking dinner for my family at night and recreating many of the recipes from my travels.

I found an undeniable sense of relief and calmness cooking dinner for my family at night and recreating many of the recipes from my travels.

Mind you, I didn't cook a whole lot when I was young—my father, a chef in the USSR army, took on that role in the family—but I certainly had exposure to constant cooking and enjoyed eating all the delicious food he made for us. You might have already guessed that, as Ukrainians, the potato—that mysterious little tuber—was a staple in our daily meals. In fact, my father had fun with potatoes in all sorts of ways: mashing them, frying them, baking them, boiling them, and roasting them, depending on what was being served. We often had mashed potatoes for dinner with a protein of some sort. And he always made great fries, any time of day.

It seemed I inherited some of his talent when I found myself making sauces during those stressful times. I made sauces for pasta, marinades for meat and fish, dressings for salads, and lots of aioli variations, infused with roasted red pepper, garlic, and chipotle pepper. I got a little obsessive about it—poring through culinary books to learn classic sauce-making techniques and trying them out in the kitchen.

Eventually, I got sick of pasta and protein as the constant base for these sauces. I thought, *What else could I use? What else would be the perfect vehicle for the flavor bomb that sauces give us in all types of cuisine?*

You guessed it: the humble, ever-versatile potato.

If you think about it, potatoes are everywhere—not only do they invariably show up alongside a burger or get stuffed with sour cream, cheese, and scallions, they also give life to all sorts of breads, desserts, and even alcohol (yes, vodka). And then there are the endless varieties and colors, from buttery Yukon Golds and fingerlings to round red potatoes, purple heirlooms, and beta carotene–rich sweet potatoes.

Around the world, this kitchen stalwart is an important part of many different cuisines and dishes, making its way into shepherd's pie, soup, and bangers and mash throughout England and Ireland; into cheesy au gratin casseroles throughout Europe; alongside sausages and mustard and beer in Germany; and dipped into kirsch-laden fondue in Switzerland. Potatoes are even a staple in northern China, where they're often served smashed and paired with garlic and truffles, not unlike in parts of France.

The be-all potato gave me an opportunity to focus on what was turning out to be my true passion: food, cooking, and dining out. I thought, *Forget about sandwiches and burgers and tacos and pizza and salads and rice bowls! What if the next great fast-casual restaurant could revolve around potatoes instead of the ubiquitous bread, tortillas, dough, and lettuce?* It made sense to me—potatoes are versatile, naturally gluten-free, unprocessed, affordable, approachable, comforting, and always craveable.

Back in my kitchen, I started pairing my signature sauces with potatoes in different forms: sliced, grated, smashed, roasted—you name it. It took me about two years of business planning before I opened my first Potatopia store in December 2011. By this time you're probably wondering why the heck I would make the leap into the restaurant industry, one of the toughest, most cutthroat businesses on the planet, when the country was going through a recession.

Let me explain. I knew the realities of the restaurant business and recognized that I had plenty of education and research to do before taking the plunge. I wanted to study everything about the restaurant business and truly learn the craft.

Over the next several months, I teamed up with the owner of a successful local sandwich shop where I was a frequent customer. He was gracious enough to allow me to shadow him at his busy restaurant. From there, I became a sponge. I asked hundreds of questions, and then, on my own time, I read industry trade material, traveled to every food and hospitality trade show I could, researched (read: ate at) countless fast-casual restaurants, and continued to shadow at other fast-casual outlets. Once I felt I had conducted a thorough market analysis of the business and gathered all the information I could about operations, efficiencies, ingredient sources, staffing, and more, I decided to try out the concept in the real world.

Using my knowledge of and contacts in the real estate business, I was able to secure some space at the Menlo Park Mall in Edison, New Jersey. It was a small space—not ideal for everything I wanted to do—but being at a mall meant I was able to serve community members from all walks of life and see what they liked and disliked. The goal was never just to open a baked potato restaurant; I wanted to open a potato haven. During the course of the first store opening, I developed almost 200 recipes. Not all could be executed at the restaurant, which is one reason you're reading a book that contains nearly 80 of those creations. But I digress.

At Potatopia, we offer our guests a line of signature potato-based, one-dish meals, including our popular Smashed Hit (seasoned smashed baby red potatoes, cheddar, Asiago, scallions, red onion, garlic, and cilantro topped with roasted red pepper aioli) and the crowd-pleasing Curly Sue, our most creative dish (curly fries, seasoned shrimp, pepper Jack and Parmesan cheeses, jalapeños, scallions, and drizzles of chipotle ketchup and garlic aioli).

Like most fast-casual restaurants, we also allow our guests to customize their meals, first by choosing a potato base (smashed, fried, baked, sweet potato crinkle, or potato chip), a protein (all-natural, hormone-, antibiotic-, and MSG-free grass-fed beef, free-range chicken, shrimp, or wood-smoked bacon), all the veggies they want, cheese (Parmesan, Asiago, or pepper Jack), and one of Potatopia's homemade sauces, such as chipotle ketchup, grainy mustard, chile pepper aioli, melted cheddar, truffle aioli, roasted red pepper aioli, and more.

Business grew steadily. In fact, it became clear that Potatopia had gained a loyal following when I noticed, day after day, the lines forming for our food. That's when I brought aboard two partners, Alex Fleyshmakher and Dimitry Meksin, and we started planning a second location, in Manhattan. That location opened in 2013 in the West Village, followed by our Staten Island Mall location in 2014.

Now, thanks in part to successful franchising agreements, Potatopia has expanded across New York and New Jersey, into Florida, and internationally in Toronto.

No day is without its successes and challenges, and I owe all that to my friend the potato. The food business is certainly the toughest in the world, but it's always a lot of fun, and I love it.

With this book, I hope to introduce you to some of the fun ways that potatoes might bring joy to your life and your kitchen as you try my recipes and experiment with different toppings and pairings, seasonings, and of course, sauces.

It turns out I have never truly given up my love of potato chips. But I've found a new version of potato heaven. Call it a Potatopia. I hope this book will help you bring a slice of this paradise into your own kitchen.

The Potato Revolution (or All About Potatoes)

I know what you're thinking. Potatoes, really? How much can you love—or do with—potatoes? But chances are you were drawn to this book for a reason. I'm guessing it was for some of the same reasons as the ones I had when I started Potatopia and decided to write this book. So many of us grew up eating potatoes as children, whether it was simple mashed potatoes, a more elaborate gratin, or the ubiquitous French fry.

But why potatoes, and why now? Why should we care?

As the fourth most popular crop in the world and a staple food on nearly every continent, it's hard to imagine how or why this nutrient-packed, clean, whole food became overrun by the now more mainstream (and more processed) options of breads, buns, tortillas, noodles, and rice. Perhaps potatoes are so ubiquitous that they're basically invisible. Many people equate them with white bread: boring, forgettable, and probably not very nutritious. This couldn't be further from the truth. So why not get reacquainted with potatoes? Here's a snapshot of some of their best traits and their culinary possibilities.

Versatile. As we've seen, there are infinite ways to prepare and cook potatoes. They can be baked, boiled, deep-fried, pan-fried, puréed, sautéed, shredded, mashed, smashed, curled, cubed, diced, and more. They can be used as a thickener in soups, dips, and sauces, or as a dough for gnocchi and dumplings. They're also the perfect base for other ingredients—the ultimate canvas for cooking creativity.

Healthy. Even though potatoes taste great fried or layered with cream and cheese in a gratin, they can be a good source of nutrition when prepared simply. In fact, they're low in calories; they are fat-, sodium-, and cholesterol-free; and they are packed with all sorts of important vitamins, minerals, and antioxidants needed for a balanced diet. They are a whole food, not processed or laden with additives and preservatives like some breads and pastas. They're also naturally gluten-free. In fact, people with celiac disease or those avoiding gluten for other reasons can use mashed or dehydrated potatoes in place of flour as a gluten-free thickener for soups, stews, and sauces, or in place of pasta when cut with a spiralizer or sliced thinly in the shape of lasagna noodles. And though potatoes are a source of carbohydrates, unlike the carbs found in most breads, cereals, and other processed starches, the carbs in potatoes are complex and slow-burning, meaning they won't raise your blood sugar as fast as processed carbs like cookies and crackers.

Sustainably grown and GMO-free. Virtually all potatoes grown in the United States are free of genetically modified organisms (GMOs) thanks to pressure from large chain restaurants, followed by several years of purging GMO strains from the certified seed pool. Even the largest of commercial potato growers use a sustainable crop rotation method, and many of America's potato farms are also family farms. According to the Washington State Potato Commission, for example, 99 percent of potato farms in the state are family farms. Additionally, small potato farms often use hand-planting and -harvesting methods.

Potato History

It is thought that potatoes were first domesticated in what is now Peru and Bolivia, where the Inca in the region cultivated wild versions of the crop, not only to eat but also to heal cuts and wounds, prevent indigestion, treat frostbite or sunburn, and ease toothaches and other bodily pains. It is thought that potatoes were first farmed around 1400 BC, when burgeoning agricultural communities discovered that potatoes' hardiness could stand up better to the erratic temperatures and terrain of the Peruvian mountains than other crops like wheat and corn.

By the 15th century, potatoes appeared in Europe, likely from gold-seeking Spanish explorers returning home from South America. The high vitamin C content of their collected tubers helped ward off scurvy as they sailed back. Eventually, potatoes spread across the continent as farmers found them easier to grow and cultivate than other crops. According to Potatoes USA, the potato became extremely popular in France in the 18th century during the reign of King Louis XIV, after a French physician named Antoine Parmentier created a feast for him using only potatoes and spoke highly of their nutritional benefits. Benjamin Franklin, ambassador to France, was in attendance at Parmentier's feast in 1767.

Still, it's been said that the first European potatoes arrived in the American colonies in 1621 when Nathaniel Butler, governor of Bermuda, sent them with other vegetables to Virginia. By the 1700s, they became more widely cultivated as a way to feed the growing population more easily and with a staple crop that could store for long periods of time. In the 1800s, Irish immigrants made potatoes popular again by introducing new varieties to the United States, where many immigrated because of the widespread famine that had spread across Ireland as a result of a potato blight.

Idaho began growing potatoes in 1836, when missionaries who had moved out West began to teach native tribes to grow crops rather than hunt and gather food. In 1872, horticulturist Luther Burbank accidentally discovered the russet potato while trying to develop a more disease-resistant potato to help Ireland deal with its famine. From there, potatoes continued on their path toward ubiquitous popularity, even being traded for gold during the Alaskan gold rush in the late 1800s because of their high vitamin C content.

In October 1995, the potato became the first vegetable to be grown in space. Today, the United States is the fifth largest producer of potatoes worldwide.

Growing Potatoes

With optimal climate and soil, modern equipment, and new technologies, US potato growers harvest an average of 20 million metric tons of potatoes each year. Potatoes are grown throughout the United States, but some states grow more potatoes than others because of their ideal climates: long, cold winters and summers with sunny days and cool nights.

As you might have guessed, Idaho produces the most potatoes in the United States,

The Potatopia Cookbook

Digging for potatoes at Roots to River Farm in Titusville, New Jersey.

followed by Washington, Wisconsin, North Dakota, Oregon, Colorado, Minnesota, Michigan, Maine, and California.

Potato seeds are planted in the spring and most potatoes are harvested in the fall, but in some cases, potatoes are harvested year-round. This cool-season crop does best in deep, loose, and well-drained soil.

As previously mentioned, most potatoes in the United States are grown using a natural, sustainable crop rotation method, which means they are planted in the same plot of land only once every three or four years. This enhances soil fertility, makes weeding unnecessary, and helps limit the need for chemical-laden pesticides and insecticides.

Potatoes grow by developing sprouts first, and then the leaves, branches, and stolons are formed. Tubers begin to form next, bulking up with water, nutrients, and carbohydrates over the course of about three months. As the leaves turn yellow or die off, tuber growth rate slows, indicating that the potato is ready for harvest via hand-digging or automated machinery.

Potato Nutrition

Potatoes have developed a bad reputation over the years because they're most commonly associated with French fries and other carb-laden, fatty favorites like potatoes au gratin and creamy mashed potatoes—which are, of course, delicious in moderation! But, as you'll see in this book, there are other ways to consume potatoes.

You may be surprised to find out that one medium, skin-on potato contains almost half the daily recommendation for vitamin C (that's more than a tangerine or tomato); as much or more potassium than bananas, spinach, and broccoli; 10 percent of the daily recommendation for vitamin B6 (which helps with energy metabolism); and other vitamins and minerals such as thiamin, riboflavin, folate, phosphorous, iron, and zinc. Best of all, a medium, skin-on potato has only 110 calories and zero fat, zero cholesterol, and zero sodium.

Even carb-phobic eaters have come back to the humble potato as a "cleaner" source of complex carbs and fiber than processed grains, breads, pastas, and cereals. Potatoes also have a high water content, so they fill you up fast, and they're low in resistant starch, meaning they don't break down as fast as other starches and carbs, which would otherwise lead to a spike in blood sugar. Because of this, potatoes are also thought to have prebiotic properties to improve digestion and immunity and reduce inflammation in the body. One medium, skin-on potato has some protein, too, the equivalent of half a glass of milk.

Additionally, potatoes are a great source of fiber and other antioxidants, meeting 8 percent of the daily recommendation for dietary fiber (that's more than oatmeal) and providing about the same amount of free-radical fighting power as carrots, garlic, broccoli, tomatoes, and eggplant.

Last but not least, potatoes are a great source of magnesium. One medium, skin-on potato provides 48 milligrams of magnesium (16 percent of the daily recommended amount). More attention is being paid these days to the importance of magnesium in a healthy diet. As the fourth most abundant mineral found in the body, it plays a role in energy production, blood pressure regulation, nerve health, and more. Studies suggest that the majority of us do not meet the current recommended levels for magnesium, and low levels of magnesium have been associated with a number of medical conditions, including migraines, Alzheimer's disease, stroke, hypertension, and cardiovascular disease.

Now that's one powerful potato.

How to Use This Book

THE PURPOSE OF THIS BOOK is to show how versatile and creative you can be with one of the world's favorite vegetables: the potato. No culinary training or significant home cooking experience is needed.

Potatoes appeal to all types of people—from every culture, background, and age group. They show up on virtually every family dinner table, not only in America but around the world. Potatoes also appeal to all types of eaters, from the very picky to the most adventurous, from vegetarians and the most health conscious among us to those avoiding gluten because of celiac disease and sensitivities. In this book, I sought to include some traditional potato dishes, but I also wanted to revolutionize the way potatoes are prepared, thought about, and consumed through surprising—yet simple—recipes for weeknight meals, weekend splurges, midday snacks, sharable plates, and everything in between. I did this at Potatopia, and now I hope this book will inspire you to take the humble potato from the side of the plate to the center of it. The potato has always been a staple side dish for Americans, but it has the potential to take a starring role, not just be a supporting player.

For the best results, I recommend first reading the recipe from start to finish and then preparing your mise en place, or ingredients and prep work, before you begin cooking or even turn on the heat. I like to use little bowls to hold my chopped and prepped ingredients. Then, I clean up before cooking, and I always try to clean as I go. This helps save time, space, and mess in the kitchen.

Buying Potatoes

Even the most mainstream grocery store in America typically carries a wide variety of potatoes, but some higher-end and specialty stores offer a growing number of heirloom and regional varieties that can make cooking with these tubers even more fun. Farmers markets are also a great resource for finding interesting, less common types of potatoes.

There are now more than 100 types of potatoes available in the United States alone, but there are 4,000 types worldwide, according to Potatoes USA, the country's potato board. American potatoes vary in size, shape, color, taste, and texture. The recipes in this book call for several potato varieties, all of which bring unique qualities to the table. Here's a quick look at my favorites:

> There are more than 4,000 types of potatoes worldwide.

Long white potatoes. Oval in shape with thin, tan skin, these potatoes have a medium starch content and creamy texture when cooked, making them great for boiling and pan-frying because they'll hold their shape. Common varieties are Onaway, Elba, and Kennebec. There are also round white varieties (not pictured), which have a low starch content and firmer texture, making them highly versatile and able to withstand high heat and heavy cooking when made into chips or used in casseroles like scalloped potato dishes. These are sometimes referred to as "boiling potatoes."

Round red potatoes. Sometimes referred to as Red Bliss or Red Pontiac, these waxy potatoes have naturally thin, red skin and white or yellowish flesh. They have medium to low starch and a high amount of moisture. Like round white potatoes, round red potatoes are sometimes called "boiling potatoes." Round red potatoes, like other waxy potatoes, hold their shape well, which makes them ideal for roasting, steaming, or slicing and serving in salads and soups. Common varieties include Norland, Red La Soda, Cal Red, AmaRosa, Chieftain, Klondike Rose, Dakota Rose, and IdaRose. At Potatopia, we use reds for our famous smashed potatoes—baby red-skin potatoes that are marinated, roasted, smashed, and fried until crispy on the outside and soft in the middle.

Purple and blue potatoes. Purple and blue potatoes have deep-colored skin and flesh ranging from rich blue to lavender. You'll find them at some grocery stores, but they are more commonly found at farmers markets. Their moist, firm flesh retains its shape while adding colorful flair to many dishes, especially simple salads and sides, where they can really stand out. Steaming preserves their color better than roasting or frying. Types of blue and purple potatoes include Purple Peruvian, Purple Passion, Adirondack Blue, Russian Blue, and All Blue.

Fingerling potatoes

Long white potatoes

Russet/Idaho potatoes

Round red potatoes

Yellow/Yukon Gold potatoes

Purple sweet potatoes

White sweet potatoes

Purple and blue potatoes

Sweet potatoes

Japanese yams

Baby/Petite/New potatoes

Japanese yams. Also known as mountain yams, these sweet yams are root vegetables and only distantly related to potatoes. They are different from sweet potatoes in that they have a more rust-colored skin and dense, cream-colored flesh with a savory, only slightly sweet squash-like flavor.

White sweet potatoes. Less common than regular sweet potatoes, this variety is milder in flavor than the orange ones, with a softer, lighter-colored skin. When you can find them, they are great for adding a little sweetness to a traditional potato dish—or toning down the sweetness of a typical sweet potato dish.

Russet/Idaho potatoes. This is the most widely grown, popular potato in the United States. It has the highest amount of starch and the lowest moisture, making it the perfect potato for mashing, oven-roasting, and frying. The high starch content also gives russet potatoes a flour-like texture, so they are ideal for baking or using in place of flour as a thickener. The hearty brown skin has extra nutritious fiber, which helps them stay fresh for months when properly stored. Burbank and Norkotah are the most common types of russet potato, but there are many others, such as Ranger, Centennial, Clearwater, Premier, Nooksack, Yukon Gem, and Shepody.

Sweet potatoes. Technically speaking, sweet potatoes are only distantly related to potatoes, but they can be prepared in much the same way, from roasted to baked to fried. Covington is the most common variety. Grown in more temperate climates in the South, sweet potatoes shouldn't be confused with yams, which are a different tuber entirely, even though we use a play on the word at Potatopia—our I Think Therefore I Yam dish uses sweet potato crinkle-cut fries as the base for a dish with roasted antibiotic-free chicken, Asiago, Parmesan, red onions, fresh garlic, and gar-lic aioli.

Fingerling potatoes. These potatoes are named for their thin shape and size, two to four inches in length. They have a waxy texture and come in all different col-ors, such as red, orange, purple, yellow, and white. When pan-fried or roasted, they have an earthy, nutty flavor. Major types include Russian Banana, French, and Ruby Crescent. You'll likely find many heirloom and regional varieties at farmers markets.

Yellow/Yukon Gold potatoes. These golden-skinned, golden-flesh pota-toes have a mild, buttery flavor when cooked, which cuts down on the need for extra butter when preparing them. Grilling brings out this potato's sweet, slightly caramelized flavor. Yukon Gold is perhaps the most widely known yellow potato, but there are also the Sierra Gold, Huckleberry Gold, Yellow Finn, and the German Butterball potato, an heirloom variety.

Purple sweet potatoes. Only commercially available since 2006, this colorful sweet potato variety is thought to have been developed by accident by a North Carolina farmer, who ended up patenting it with the name Stokes Purple. These potatoes have a rich, almost wine-like taste and need to be cooked longer than sweet potatoes because of their denser flesh.

Baby/Petite/New potatoes. Picked in the spring or early summer, these potatoes are simply the "younger" versions of their full-grown counterparts in different colors and varieties. Since these potatoes are harvested early in their development, they usually have thin skins, a waxy texture, low starch content, and high moisture content, which helps their flesh and skin remain intact even when cooked. This makes them especially suited for salads and roasted potato dishes.

Regardless of the potatoes you are purchasing, look for clean, smooth, firm potatoes with no cuts, bruises, or discoloration. Farmers market potatoes might have a few of those, though, and that's okay. The fresh, just-harvested taste will make up for them.

Storing Potatoes

Once you purchase your potatoes and get them home, it's time to store them. If properly stored, a raw potato can last up to a year before going bad. Their heartiness is partially why potatoes have been used over the years as a staple food, especially in times of crop failures, war, and other instances of mortal peril.

Potatoes are best stored in a dark, cool, well-ventilated place, such as a pantry, cellar, or even the garage so they don't turn green and sprout. (For the record, a little sprouting and greenness is okay; just cut it away before cooking.) You can store them in paper bags, too, to shut out the light. Note that while the cabinet under the sink is a dark place, the temperatures can get too high for potatoes. Personally, I usually do not store potatoes for long periods of time, as they're the fastest moving vegetables in my house! But if you do store them for longer, be sure not to wrap them in plastic, as they can sweat and go bad fast because of the trapped moisture. I also avoid washing potatoes before storing because this can cause dampness and lead to quicker rotting. Avoid the refrigerator and freezer, too, because temperatures lower than 50°F can cause a potato's starch to convert to sugar, which can lead to discoloration when cooked.

> If properly stored, a raw potato can last up to a year before going bad.

Preparing Potatoes

All the recipes in this book assume that you are starting with clean, unpeeled potatoes unless otherwise stated. To clean potatoes before cooking, gently scrub them with a vegetable brush under cool, running water. Leaving the skins on will help preserve some of their nutrients and add extra texture to a dish, so I leave them on most of the time.

However, a peeled potato works better in certain recipes. I use a simple vegetable peeler to peel potatoes. When you peel potatoes, immediately place them in a bowl of cool water; otherwise they can turn brown, just like apples, thanks to the sugars in the potato reacting with the oxygen in the air. You can add a little lemon juice or vinegar to the water to be extra cautious. If the potatoes do become discolored, they're still safe to eat—they just don't look as nice.

Be aware that putting the potatoes in water can cut down on their high starch content, which you want for dishes like gratins, casseroles, and potato salads. In those cases, just try to work as fast as you can to slice and cook them to prevent discoloration. You can also slice them and marinate them in a little olive oil.

The recipes in this book call for a variety of knife cuts. Sometimes it's best to cut potatoes into equal-size cubes, shoestrings, or wedges so they cook evenly when roasting or frying. Other recipes call for a mandoline or very sharp knife to thinly slice potatoes for chips. Here are some of the most popular knife cuts you can use when working with potatoes, although not all of these are called for in this cookbook:

Spiralize. You can purchase a spiralizer tool from most stores where kitchen goods are sold. While I don't use this tool very often, it's fun to take it out and create a pasta-like shape out of potatoes as a base for different toppings and sauces. You can also use it for making curly fries. If you want to experiment, try substituting these curly fries for the shoestrings in Reuben-Style Shoestring Cheese Fries (page 54) or Shoestring Fries with Spiced Shrimp (page 49)!

Dice. This shape is perfect not only for soups and sautéed dishes where you want the potatoes to appear evenly shaped, but also for recipes where you want to make sure the potatoes cook evenly. Cutting the dice to about the same size and shape will help them cook at the same speed so you don't end up with a mix of some mushy potatoes and some less-cooked hard pieces. While it might seem challenging to cut round potatoes into perfect cubes, all it takes is a little practice. First, slice off the ends of the potato and then the sides so you end up with a long rectangle. (Save the scraps for soups.) Then, slice the potato lengthwise into ¼-inch-thick "planks." Working in batches, stack a few planks on top of each other and slice them first lengthwise and then crosswise into cubes.

> Cutting the dice to about the same size and shape will help them cook at the same speed so you don't end up with a mix of some mushy potatoes and some less-cooked hard pieces.

Thick-cut. This shape works great for homemade fries. I like to leave some of the skin on the potato because it gives the fries a more rustic, homemade feel and a heartier taste. To create this shape, cut the potatoes lengthwise into ½-inch-thick slices, stack them, and then cut them again lengthwise into ½-inch-thick fries.

Shoestring. This is a thinner cut for fries, sometimes referred to as a matchstick cut, but for consistency, we'll stick with shoestring. To make it, cut the potatoes lengthwise into ⅛-inch-thick slices using a mandoline or very sharp knife. Then stack the slices and cut them lengthwise again into ¼-inch-thick strips. Finally, cut them in half crosswise to make shorter fries.

Flat spiralize. Most spiralizers have varying thickness in cuts. The one used here makes a continuous flat spiral, similar to those "hurricane potato chips on a stick" popular on East Coast boardwalks. If you want to have some fun with presentation, try using this cut to make the Beer-Battered Sweet Potato Chips with Ranch Dip (page 35); the longer, spiralized pieces are ideal for dipping and crunching away.

Slice. When you are making chips, it's important to have very thin, uniform potato slices so they cook quickly and evenly. I recommend a roughly ⅛-inch-thick slice for making potato chips. A mandoline makes this kind of prep easy. Many mandolines come with a prop so they will rest at a 45-degree angle on your chopping board. That way you can just hold the mandoline steady with one hand and run the potato over the blade in a sweeping motion, not back and forth. If you don't have a mandoline, it's possible to make thin slices using a super sharp knife. (A too-dull knife presents a hazard for cutting yourself.)

Wedge. Wedges are great for roasting because the outsides will get crispy and caramelized but the potato flesh stays tender. To make them, halve the potatoes lengthwise, then slice the halves lengthwise on the diagonal to create wedges.

Hash. This shape is great for making crispy hash browns. To make it, simply grate potatoes using a box grater. Make sure to pat the potatoes dry after grating to remove moisture before you start cooking.

Ripple. None of the recipes in the book call for this potato cut since it's difficult to do at home without the right tools, but we use this shape often at Potatopia for our chips. Some mandolines have a blade adapter that can be used to make this ripple pattern, which is better for thinner chips. There are also special corrugated knives that can cut potatoes into chips like this. If you're able to create this shape, you can use it for the Black and White Chocolate-Covered Potato Chips (page 158) because the ripple shape will hold the chocolate better. Or try it in a savory dish, such as the Golden Potato Chips with Spanish Ham (page 48) or Sushi Tuna and Salmon Tartare Chips (page 62).

Spiralize

Dice

Slice

Flat spiralize

Ripple

Hash

Thick-cut

Shoestring

Wedge

Popular knife cuts

Some dishes work best with potatoes that are cut into certain shapes and sizes, which affects how they cook and work with other ingredients. Understanding these knife cuts (see page 22) will set you up for success in the kitchen.

Cooking Potatoes

Potatoes can be cooked in just about any way imaginable. I prefer to cook potatoes on the stovetop or in the oven rather than in the microwave, as microwaving can damage some of the potato's natural nutrients.

Boiling. Put the potatoes and about ¼ cup salt in a pot and add enough cold water to cover them by about two inches. Bring the water to a boil and immediately reduce to a simmer. The reason I recommend starting with cold water is because if you add potatoes to boiling water, they will cook unevenly. It's best to bring the potatoes and water to a boil together and then reduce to a simmer so they don't overcook and break apart. Just as with pasta, when boiling potatoes, I reserve some of the cooking water and add a little back to mashed potatoes or soups because its starch content helps bind the potatoes with the other ingredients. And though it seems like you're adding a lot of salt when boiling, only some of the salt gets into the potatoes—just enough to flavor them perfectly.

Roasting. Potatoes can be cut into cubes or wedges to roast. The important thing is that they are all the same size and shape so they cook evenly. Coat them in olive oil and make sure they are about ½ inch apart on the baking sheet before popping them in a 450°F oven.

Steaming. You can use a stainless steel steamer insert in your pot or even a bamboo steamer to steam potatoes. Steaming, rather than boiling, helps make potatoes tender without getting too mushy.

Deep-frying. Depending on how many people you are serving, you can use a small countertop electric fryer—they are very inexpensive and sold in any major home retailer—but this works best when you're cooking for more than four people. Otherwise, I use a four- to six-quart enameled cast iron pot. I like to fry potatoes in rice bran oil since it's non-GMO, nonallergenic, and neutral tasting. You can also use pure duck fat, which gives the fries a little something extra. If you cannot find either, use canola oil or any other polyunsaturated vegetable oil with a high smoke point. Always use enough oil to fully submerge the potatoes—usually four to six inches will do, but be sure to leave at least two inches from the top of the pot to protect yourself from splashes. Before frying, make sure the oil is at least 350° to 375°F. In addition to checking with a deep-fry thermometer, you can also tell that the oil is hot enough when it shimmers. Remember to fry in small batches so you do not crowd the pot; otherwise, your fries and chips will be soggy. Check the oil's temperature between batches, increasing the heat as necessary to ensure that the oil remains at the ideal temperature. If the oil isn't hot enough, your potatoes may be greasy and/or undercooked. To keep fries and chips crisp while working in batches, quickly drain them on a paper towel, immediately season them (so the seasoning sticks to the hot potatoes), transfer them to a baking sheet, and hold them in a 200°F oven until all the fries or chips have been cooked. If the oil is still clear after frying, you can let it cool before straining through a fine-mesh sieve. Save it for the next time you fry!

Pan-frying. Pan-frying in butter, rice bran oil, or another neutral vegetable oil is a great alternative to deep-frying, especially for thicker fries. It is easier than managing all that hot oil, and you don't have to work in as many batches. I prefer butter when pan-frying potatoes because it coats the potatoes better than oil and feels less greasy. When pan-frying with butter, you do have to be careful that the butter does not start to burn, as it will sizzle fast and splash when you add the potatoes. You want a nice, small, bubbly sizzle when you add the potatoes.

Unless otherwise specified, I have tested all the recipes in this book with regular table salt. If you prefer to cook with coarser salt, like sea salt or kosher salt, note that you may need to use more than the recipe calls for, since table salt is the most potent of the three. I also use freshly ground black pepper instead of preground black pepper for a brighter taste, and I like Greek olive oil best for its mild, buttery flavor and gentle aroma.

Everyone always asks me, "What condiments should I have on hand for potatoes, other than just ketchup?" Of course there are many sauces, dressings, and marinades you can make for potatoes (see Appendix B, page 173), but when it comes to basic condiments, I like mustard, vinegar, and hot sauce. You can use a wide variety of spices, too, as you might have guessed. I always keep garlic powder (not garlic salt), onion powder, cayenne pepper, and red pepper flakes on hand, as well as breadcrumbs for casserole-type potato dishes. (I don't like to use garlic salt because I prefer to have more control over the salt added to the recipes.)

Preserving Potatoes

After enjoying your delicious potato dish, refrigerate leftovers in an airtight container within two hours and store them for no longer than a few days. I prefer not to freeze cooked potatoes at home because they can get really watery when reheated. After all, potatoes are 80 percent water.

Let's get cooking!

CHAPTER 1:
Starters
and Snacks

Potatoes can be eaten at any meal or at any time of day—for breakfast, as an afternoon bite, as an appetizer to a larger meal, or even as part of a dessert! For this chapter, do with these dishes what you will—eat them for a quick, sharable snack, serve them as part of an entertaining spread, or combine them for a larger multicourse meal. Some of the recipes have extra protein, making these "starters" also fitting for small meals by themselves.

Sweet and Savory Maple-Glazed Potato Chips with Bacon

This dish was a delicious accident. While working on the menu for our Potatopia Canada stores, we were brainstorming what to do with maple syrup—an important food produced by our neighbor. As we ate our way through Toronto, we noticed maple and bacon paired together quite often on pizza. We thought, *Why not try those ingredients with potatoes?* This satisfying snack or starter has our two favorite tastes—sweet and savory—in one. For even more umami flavor, swap the salt for grated Parmesan cheese.

SERVES 2

1 large russet potato, peeled
Rice bran or other neutral vegetable oil,
    for frying
4 slices bacon

2 tablespoons unsalted butter
⅓ cup pure maple syrup
1 tablespoon light brown sugar
Pinch sea salt

1. Using a mandoline or very sharp knife, cut the potato lengthwise into paper-thin slices. Submerge the slices in a large bowl of water and refrigerate for 6 to 8 hours.

2. In a large Dutch oven, heat 3 inches of oil over medium heat until it shimmers and a deep-fry thermometer registers 375°F. Remove the potato slices from the bowl of water and dry them completely between paper towels. Add half of the potato slices to the oil and fry, moving them around with tongs to make sure they do not overcook, for about 2 minutes, or until the chips are golden brown. Repeat with the remaining half, making sure the oil is back up to temperature before frying. Reduce the heat if the chips brown too fast. Transfer the chips to paper towels to drain and cool.

3. Cook the bacon in a large skillet over medium heat until crisp, 4 to 5 minutes per side. Transfer to paper towels to drain. Reserve ½ teaspoon of the bacon drippings.

4. In a small saucepan, melt the butter over medium heat until the foaming subsides. Add the syrup, brown sugar, and reserved bacon drippings. Cook, whisking occasionally, for about 3 minutes, or until bubbly. Remove from the heat.

5. Put the chips in a large metal bowl and drizzle the warm syrup glaze all over them. Sprinkle on the salt and toss to coat well. Chop or crumble the bacon and scatter it over the chips. Serve immediately.

Aligot Croquettes

These croquettes are a tasty extension of the aligot recipe in chapter 6. Aligot is a classic, fondue-like French dish made by adding cheese—often creamy Gruyère and/or mozzarella—to mashed potatoes. When breaded and deep-fried, these croquettes make a great addition to a dinner party or other food-driven get-together.

MAKES 15-20 CROQUETTES

1 large egg

1 cup seasoned dry breadcrumbs, plus more as needed

Rice bran or other neutral vegetable oil, for frying

1 recipe Aligot (page 142)

Thinly sliced scallions, both green and white parts, for garnish

Sour cream, for dipping

1. Beat the egg in a shallow bowl. Spread the breadcrumbs in another shallow bowl. In a medium saucepan, heat 2 inches of oil over medium heat until it shimmers and a deep-fry thermometer registers 375°F.

2. While the oil heats, prepare the aligot croquettes. Spoon 1 tablespoon of the aligot into your hands and roll it into a ball, and then roll it into a cylinder. Repeat this process until all the aligot is used up. Roll a croquette in the beaten egg and use a fork to drain off the excess egg. Transfer the croquette to the breadcrumbs and use the fork to roll it until well coated. Set aside on a rimmed baking sheet. Repeat this process with the remaining croquettes.

3. Working in batches so as not to crowd the pan, add about 5 croquettes to the oil and fry for 1 to 2 minutes, until golden brown. Stir the croquettes with tongs to prevent them from sticking together. Using a slotted spoon, transfer the croquettes to paper towels to drain. Allow the oil to regain temperature between batches.

4. Serve the croquettes on a platter or in a large shallow bowl. Garnish with scallions and offer sour cream on the side for dipping.

Beer-Battered Sweet Potato Chips with Ranch Dip

Beer and potato chips are a natural combination, with the hoppy bubbles of your favorite brew washing down your favorite salty snack. But have you tried beer with sweet potato chips? Now there's another flavor dimension to the perfect pairing: earthy sweetness. My ranch dip, always a house staple, balances everything out with some extra creamy tang.

MAKES 20–25 CHIPS

Flour Mixture
2 cups all-purpose flour
1½ tablespoons granulated garlic
1 tablespoon salt
1 teaspoon freshly ground black pepper
1 teaspoon paprika
1 teaspoon Old Bay seasoning

Batter
¾ cup all-purpose flour
1 teaspoon freshly ground black pepper

½ teaspoon salt
2 large egg yolks
3 cups beer (pick your favorite)

Sweet Potato Chips
Rice bran or other neutral vegetable oil, for frying
1 large sweet potato, peeled and rinsed
Chopped fresh flat-leaf parsley, for garnish (optional)
1 recipe Ranch Dip (page 174)

1. **For the flour mixture:** Combine all the ingredients in a large shallow bowl, mix well, and set aside.

2. **For the batter:** Combine all the ingredients in a deep bowl, mix well, and set aside.

3. **For the sweet potato chips:** In a large saucepan, heat 3 inches of oil over medium heat until it shimmers and a deep-fry thermometer registers 375°F.

4. While the oil heats, use a mandoline or very sharp knife to cut the sweet potato into ⅛-inch-thick slices. One at a time, dip a slice into the flour mixture, coating each side. Next, dip the slice into the batter, coating well. Return the slice to the flour mixture, again coating well. Transfer the battered potato slice to a rimmed baking sheet and repeat the process with the remaining potato slices.

5. Working in batches so as not to crowd the pan, add about 5 battered potato slices to the oil and fry for 3 to 4 minutes, until they are just golden. Stir the potato slices with tongs to prevent them from sticking together. Using a slotted spoon, transfer the potato slices to paper towels to drain. Allow the oil to regain temperature between batches.

6. Garnish with parsley, if desired, and serve immediately with the ranch dip.

Brined Potato Burger Sliders with Spicy Sesame Aioli

Why do you need a processed bun when you can make a better one out of a potato? Brining the potato slices first in seasoning and herbs helps bump up the flavor profile overall. Think of these sliders as if the fries have become the bread for the burger!

MAKES 8 SLIDERS

2 large russet potatoes
3 cloves garlic, peeled
3 fresh thyme sprigs
3 fresh sage leaves
2 bay leaves
2 tablespoons granulated sugar
1 tablespoon salt
1 tablespoon whole black peppercorns
3–4 cups ice cubes
8 ounces ground beef

8 ounces ground veal
Salt and freshly ground black pepper, to taste
3–4 tablespoons rice bran or other neutral vegetable oil, for frying
8 small iceberg lettuce leaves
2 Roma or other small tomatoes, thinly sliced
1 recipe Spicy Sesame Aioli (page 174)

1. Put the potatoes in a large saucepan and add enough cold water to cover them by 2 inches. Remove the potatoes and set them aside. Add the garlic, thyme, sage, bay leaves, sugar, salt, and peppercorns to the water and bring to a boil over high heat.

2. While the brine is cooking, cut the potatoes crosswise into ¼-inch-thick slices, discarding the end pieces. As soon as the brine reaches a boil, remove the pan from the heat and add the ice. Put the potato slices in the brine, cover, and refrigerate for at least 12 hours or up to 3 days.

3. Preheat the oven to 375°F. Grease a rimmed baking sheet.

4. Remove the potato slices from the brine and place them in a single layer on the prepared baking sheet. Discard the brine. Bake for 15 minutes. Turn the slices over and continue to bake for another 10 to 12 minutes, until the edges start to crisp and brown.

5. While the potatoes are cooking, combine the ground beef and veal, mixing well. Shape the meat into 2-ounce slider patties, taking care to keep them the same diameter as the potatoes. Season lightly with salt and pepper.

6. In a large skillet or cast iron pan, heat the rice bran oil over medium-high heat until it shimmers. Add the patties and cook for 2 to 3 minutes per side for medium doneness, or longer for your preferred doneness.

7. Place a potato slice on a plate and place a patty on top. Top with a lettuce leaf and a slice of tomato. Spread the aioli on a second potato slice and place it on top of the slider. Repeat this process to assemble the rest of the sliders. Serve immediately.

The Potatopia Cookbook

Cheddar and Gruyère Fondue with Crispy Potato Wedges

When I'm at a restaurant and there's an option for cheese fries, I always go for it. This recipe is a more flavorful—and perhaps more sophisticated—way to spread the love of cheese fries around with crispy oven-roasted potato wedges dipped in a classic fondue with wine, Gruyère, and a little sharp cheddar. Less mess, more fun.

SERVES 4-6

Potatoes

6 medium russet potatoes

1 tablespoon canola oil

¼ cup plain dry breadcrumbs, plus more for garnish

2 teaspoons chopped fresh chives, plus more for garnish

1 teaspoon celery salt

1 teaspoon paprika

½ teaspoon chopped fresh rosemary

¼ teaspoon garlic powder

Fondue

1 clove garlic, lightly smashed

1 cup dry white wine, such as Sauvignon Blanc or Pinot Grigio, plus more as needed

8 ounces sharp cheddar, shredded

8 ounces Gruyère, shredded

1 tablespoon cornstarch

1 tablespoon freshly squeezed lemon juice

Kosher salt and freshly ground white pepper, to taste

1. Preheat the oven to 400°F. Grease a rimmed baking sheet and set aside.

2. **For the potatoes:** Cut each potato lengthwise into 8 wedges. In a large bowl, toss the potato wedges with the oil to lightly coat. Combine the breadcrumbs, chives, celery salt, paprika, rosemary, and garlic powder in a small bowl. Add the breadcrumb mixture to the wedges and toss to coat well. Transfer to the prepared baking sheet and bake for 35 to 40 minutes, until crisp and golden brown.

3. **For the fondue:** While the potatoes are cooking, rub the garlic inside the top part of a double boiler. Discard the garlic. Pour about 2 inches of water in the bottom part of the double boiler and bring to a simmer over high heat. Reduce the heat to medium-low to maintain a gentle simmer and place the top of the double boiler on top, taking care not to let it touch the simmering water. Add the wine and heat until it steams.

4. While the wine is heating, toss together the cheddar, Gruyère, and cornstarch in a bowl until evenly coated.

5. Once the wine is steaming, add the cheese mixture, a handful at a time, stirring constantly with a wooden spoon until everything is melted before adding more. The whole process should take 8 to 10 minutes, but do not let the cheese simmer; reduce the heat if necessary and be sure to stir constantly. Remove the fondue dip from the heat and stir in the lemon juice. Season with salt and pepper. If the fondue starts to firm up too much, stir in a splash of wine to loosen it; you are looking for a consistency similar to a thick sauce.

6. To serve, garnish the fondue with chives and breadcrumbs. Set the pan of fondue in the middle of a platter and assemble the cooked potatoes around it for dipping.

Allen's Tip:
Avoid using preshredded cheddar since those products are often coated with potato starch and will prevent the cheese from melting as well as it could. Stick to a classic brick of sharp cheddar that you slice yourself.

Potato and Caramelized Onion Stuffed Cronish

The popularity of the cronut, a cross between a croissant and a doughnut, inspired me to create the cronish. My creation crosses a croissant with a knish, an Eastern European stuffed dough snack. Ideally, the proper way to make a cronish would be to make croissant dough, but that is very labor-intensive. Store-bought dough is just as delicious for this recipe. Promise.

MAKES 8 CRONISHES

2 medium russet potatoes or large Yukon Gold potatoes, peeled and rinsed
2 tablespoons olive oil
½ medium yellow onion, sliced
2 tablespoons unsalted butter, at room temperature

Salt and freshly ground black pepper, to taste
1 (8-ounce) tube refrigerated crescent roll dough, separated into 8 triangles

1. Put the potatoes in a large saucepan and add enough cold salted water to cover them by 2 inches. Bring to a boil over high heat. Reduce the heat to medium and simmer for about 15 minutes, until a sharp knife easily pierces the potatoes. Drain the potatoes in a colander.

2. In a large skillet, heat the olive oil over medium heat. Add the onion and sauté for 5 to 7 minutes, until the edges are browned and caramelized. Add the whole potatoes and use a potato masher to mash the potatoes in the skillet. Add the butter and continue mashing to the desired consistency, stirring to coat the potatoes with the onion. Season with salt and pepper. Stir, remove from the heat, and set aside to cool to room temperature.

3. Preheat the oven to 350°F.

4. Lay out the crescent roll dough triangles on a clean work surface. Place 1 heaping tablespoon of the mashed potato mixture on the short side of 1 triangle and roll the dough over to the far point of the triangle. Make sure to tuck and gently pull the dough to cover the mixture. Bend the ends to form a crescent shape and place it on a rimmed baking sheet. Repeat with the remaining triangles.

5. Bake for 8 to 10 minutes, until the dough rises and turns golden brown. Serve warm or at room temperature.

Truffled Eggplant-Stuffed Potato Skins

For a spin on traditional potato skins, try this vegetable-stuffed version for a lighter treat. And vegetarians? Look no further than this recipe when you need a just-as-satisfying party starter. The white truffle oil makes the skins extra special, but if you don't have it on hand, a good-quality olive oil will also work.

SERVES 8

3 tablespoons extra virgin olive oil, divided
1½ tablespoons white truffle oil, divided
1 tablespoon Tuscan seasoning or Italian seasoning
4 large russet potatoes
2 large purple eggplants, peeled and cubed
1 green bell pepper, seeded, membranes removed, and chopped
1 red bell pepper, seeded, membranes removed, and chopped

1 ripe tomato, cored and cubed
1 celery rib, chopped
1 shallot, minced
1 clove garlic, minced
Salt and freshly ground black pepper, to taste
1 large egg
¾–1 cup shredded Parmesan (2–3 ounces)
¾ cup ricotta
1 teaspoon chopped fresh chives

1. Preheat the oven to 375°F.

2. In a small bowl, stir together 1 tablespoon of the olive oil, 1 tablespoon of the truffle oil, and the Tuscan seasoning. Brush the oil mixture all over the potatoes and place them on a rimmed baking sheet. Bake for about 1 hour, or until a sharp knife easily pierces the potatoes. Set them aside to cool for 15 minutes; keep the oven on.

3. While the potatoes bake and cool, combine the eggplants, bell peppers, tomato, and celery in a large bowl and toss.

4. In a 12-inch skillet, heat the remaining 2 tablespoons of olive oil over medium-high heat. Add the shallot and garlic and cook for 2 to 3 minutes, until the shallot softens. Take care that the garlic does not burn. Add the vegetable mixture and cook, stirring occasionally, for 5 to 6 minutes, until they begin to soften. Season with salt and pepper. Return the vegetables to the large bowl and let them cool slightly.

5. Lightly whisk the egg and pour it over the slightly cooled vegetables, mixing well. (If the vegetables are too hot, the egg will cook.)

6. Halve the potatoes lengthwise. Using a paring knife, cut around the edges of the potato halves ¼ inch from the edges. Scoop the center of the potatoes into a bowl, leaving the shells intact, and set aside the flesh for another use.

7. Carefully spoon the vegetables into the potato skins and place them, filled sides up, on the baking sheet. Sprinkle each with the Parmesan and return them to the oven. Bake for 8 to 10 minutes, until the filling is heated through and the cheese melts. To brown them, raise the oven temperature to 500°F or turn on the broiler for 2 to 3 minutes.

8. In a small bowl, whisk together the ricotta, the remaining ½ tablespoon of truffle oil, and the chives. Season with salt. Spoon the ricotta topping onto the potato skins and serve.

"Everything Bagel" Potato Croquettes

These bites of potato goodness are coated with all the delicious flavors of one of my favorite New York indulgences, an everything bagel: garlic, onion, poppy seeds, sesame seeds, and coarse salt. This is where the similarity to bagels ends and the potato part begins: you roll cheesy mashed potatoes into balls, coat them with everything, and bake them to a golden turn. Serve these as a first course, finger food at a party, bite-size snack, or even a small meal with a green salad.

MAKES 8–10 CROQUETTES

2 cups Creamy Mashed Potatoes (page 166), chilled

¾ cup shredded Emmentaler (about 2 ounces)

½ cup all-purpose flour

1 large egg

1 cup plain dry breadcrumbs or panko

2 tablespoons minced dried garlic (not granulated)

2 tablespoons minced dried onion

2 tablespoons poppy seeds

2 tablespoons sesame seeds

2 teaspoons coarse sea salt

1. Preheat the oven to 350°F. Lightly grease a rimmed baking sheet.

2. In a medium bowl, stir together the mashed potatoes and Emmentaler.

3. Put the flour in a shallow bowl. In another shallow bowl, whisk the egg well. In a third shallow bowl, combine the breadcrumbs, dried garlic, dried onion, poppy seeds, sesame seeds, and salt and mix well.

4. Using a soup spoon or tablespoon, scoop some of the potato mixture from the bowl and use your hands to gently mold it into a ball about the size of a golf ball. Repeat until you have used the entire mixture; you should get 8 to 10 balls. Roll 1 potato ball in the flour until coated and then dip it in the egg. It may fall apart a little at this point. Keeping the ball's shape as best you can, roll it in the seasonings, reforming it into a ball as you do so. Set the croquette on the prepared baking sheet. Repeat this process with the remaining ingredients.

5. Bake the croquettes for 5 minutes. Turn them over and continue to bake for 2 to 3 minutes, until the croquettes are lightly browned and heated through. Take care that the bottoms of the croquettes don't burn. Serve immediately.

Allen's Tip: Emmentaler is a Swiss cheese, so you can substitute any cheese labeled "Swiss cheese" for this recipe. You can also choose any cheese that has a nutty, sweet taste and firm, never rubbery texture.

Mashed Potato Bacon Bites with Hot Ginger Sauce

When I was a kid, I had the habit of stopping at a local Chinese restaurant to buy an egg roll or two to snack on. I just couldn't get enough of the exterior's crispy texture and the interior's soft, tasty filling. I guess it's not surprising that I decided to fill wonton wrappers with potatoes and crumbled bacon to make my own version. Because these are Asian in spirit, I like to serve them with a hot, gingery dipping sauce. The first time I made these, my five-year-old was enchanted. He liked them so much that we kept filling and rolling the wontons until we had so many we had to share them with the neighbors!

MAKES 18–20 BITES

5 slices bacon
2 cups Creamy Mashed Potatoes (page 166), chilled
18–20 (4-inch square) wonton wrappers
Rice bran or other neutral vegetable oil, for frying

Chopped scallions or fresh chives, for garnish
1 recipe Hot Ginger Sauce (page 175), for serving

1. In a large skillet, cook the bacon over medium-high heat, turning occasionally, until crisp. Transfer the bacon to paper towels to drain and cool. When cool enough to handle, crumble or chop the bacon into small pieces. In a medium bowl, combine the mashed potatoes and bacon bits.

2. Lay 1 wonton wrapper on a work surface and spoon about 1 tablespoon of the potato mixture in the middle. With the tip of your finger, rub some cold water on the edges of the wrapper. Fold the bottom and sides of the wrapper over the potato mixture. Then fold the top down, making an envelope. Repeat this process with the remaining wonton wrappers and filling.

3. In a deep skillet, heat ½ inch of oil over medium-high heat until it shimmers and a deep-fry thermometer registers 360°F.

4. Working in batches so as not to crowd the pan, add a few wrapped bacon bites and fry for about 1 minute on each side. Stir the bacon bites with tongs to prevent them from sticking together. Using a slotted spoon, transfer the bites to paper towels to drain. Allow the oil to regain temperature between batches.

5. Transfer the bites to a serving platter. Garnish with scallions and serve with the dipping sauce.

Allen's Tip: **Wonton wrappers are sold in the refrigerated section of the supermarket and may be round or square. Square wrappers, which I use here, measure 4 inches, while round wrappers are only about 3 inches in diameter. Larger egg roll wrappers are 6 inches square, which is the only difference between wonton and egg roll wrappers.**

Hatch Chile Poppers with Cheesy Mashed Potatoes

Hatch chiles, grown primarily in New Mexico, are unique in that they are available for only three weeks out of the year. Travel through the Southwest during September and you'll catch the smell of these green gems roasting away outside restaurants, supermarkets, farms, and backyards (roasting reduces the sharpness of their heat). Locals bring entire sacks of the roasted chiles home to seed, chop, and preserve in sauces, cans, and jars to last them throughout the year. You might be lucky enough to get your hands on a few Hatch chiles in season at a Latin or other specialty grocery store, but if you can't find them, try large jalapeños for a just-as-spicy kick, or milder poblano chiles.

SERVES 6

4 small russet potatoes, peeled, rinsed, and quartered

¼ (18- to 20-inch) fresh baguette, torn into several pieces

3 tablespoons Parmesan

½ teaspoon salt, plus more to taste

½ teaspoon freshly ground black pepper, plus more to taste

6 tablespoons unsalted butter, 2 tablespoons melted and 4 tablespoons at room temperature

¼ cup heavy cream, gently heated

½ cup shredded mild cheddar

¾ cup homemade or Hormel bacon bits (optional)

3 large Hatch chiles, halved lengthwise and seeded

1 tablespoon olive oil

1. Preheat the oven to 325°F.

2. Put the potatoes in a large saucepan and add enough cold salted water to cover them by 2 inches. Bring to a boil over high heat. Reduce the heat to medium and simmer for about 15 minutes, or until a sharp knife easily pierces the potatoes.

3. Meanwhile, combine the baguette, Parmesan, salt, and pepper in the bowl of a food processor. Pulse to form coarse breadcrumbs. Stir in the melted butter.

4. Drain the potatoes and return them to the pot. Add the room-temperature butter and mash, adding the warm cream, cheddar, and bacon bits (if using). Season with salt and pepper as needed.

5. Line up the chile halves, cut side up, on a rimmed baking sheet. Drizzle the olive oil over the chiles and rub to coat the insides. Fill each chile half with the mashed potatoes. Divide the breadcrumb mixture evenly over the potatoes.

6. Bake for 15 to 20 minutes, until the tops are golden brown. Let the chile poppers cool for 3 to 5 minutes before serving.

Allen's Tip: **The mashed potatoes can be made the day before and refrigerated in an airtight container.**

Golden Potato Chips with Spanish Ham (p. 48)

Golden Potato Chips with Spanish Ham

I was first introduced to Spanish Ibérico ham at a restaurant trade show. I immediately loved the mild, smoky, buttery flavor. One night, when hosting a football watching party, instead of topping my Golden Potato Chips with the usual crispy bacon, I used Ibérico ham, which made the chips a little more elegant and flavorful. When frying the chips, rice bran, canola, or other vegetable oil works just fine, but if you can find duck fat (typically available at a specialty grocery store), adding a couple tablespoons of that liquid gold bumps up the rich flavor even more.

SERVES 2–4

4 thin slices Spanish-style ham, such as Ibérico, finely chopped
½ cup pine nuts
1 recipe Golden Potato Chips (page 167)
Finely grated Manchego or Parmesan
Chopped fresh flat-leaf parsley

1. Heat a nonstick skillet over medium heat. Add the ham and cook, using a wooden spoon to separate the pieces into a single layer, until the edges begin to crisp, 2 to 3 minutes. Transfer the ham to paper towels to drain. Add the pine nuts to the fat in the skillet and sauté them until just golden brown, 2 to 3 minutes. Transfer the pine nuts to a bowl.

2. Put the potato chips in a serving bowl and sprinkle generously with Manchego. Toss lightly to coat. Scatter the ham, pine nuts, and parsley over the chips and serve immediately.

Shoestring Fries with Spiced Shrimp

My son loves shrimp cocktail but hates the store-bought versions. I've gotten into the habit of buying fresh shrimp and making my own appetizer for him. One day we decided to switch things up a bit and came up with the idea of dipping shoestring fries into our cocktail sauce instead. But we missed the shrimp, so we threw that back in with some seasoning. The spiciness of the shrimp works well with the crunchy potatoes, and the Gouda melts well and adds a smoky nuttiness to the dish.

SERVES 4

5 cups water
2 teaspoons rice vinegar
2 tablespoons Old Bay seasoning
1 tablespoon red pepper flakes
1 teaspoon chili powder
1 teaspoon salt
2 bay leaves

1 pound jumbo shrimp (about 20), peeled and deveined
1 recipe Shoestring Fries (page 169)
¼ cup shredded smoked Gouda
3 tablespoons chopped fresh chives
8 lemon wedges
1 cup cocktail sauce

1. In a large saucepan, combine the water, rice vinegar, Old Bay, red pepper flakes, chili powder, salt, and bay leaves. Bring the mixture to a boil over high heat, stirring occasionally. Add the shrimp and cook for 2 to 3 minutes, just until the shrimp are opaque. Drain the shrimp in a colander and discard the bay leaves.

2. Divide the fries among 4 serving plates. Top them with the Gouda and chives. Place 5 shrimp on each plate and garnish with 2 lemon wedges. Serve with the cocktail sauce for dipping.

Jersey Sweet Potato Chips with Steak Tartare

When traveling in Paris years ago, I got hooked on tartare, always starting a meal with it. In Paris, you'll find the raw beef dish served with a raw egg yolk on top that you break table-side and mix in with the meat. If you want to do the same for your guests as a presentation trick, just leave one of the yolks out of the mixture and place it on top of the mound when serving. For the chips, sweet potatoes make a fine balance with the richness of the beef and eggs. I like to use Jersey sweets, which are thin-skinned, white-fleshed, and not quite as sweet or moist as the typical orange sweet potatoes.

SERVES 4

1 pound lean ground beef, such as sirloin or tenderloin

4 large egg yolks

½ medium red onion, finely chopped

2 tablespoons chopped fresh flat-leaf parsley, plus more for garnish

2 anchovies in oil, drained and minced

1 tablespoon drained capers, minced

1 tablespoon Dijon mustard

⅓ cup extra virgin olive oil

Salt and freshly ground black pepper, to taste

1 recipe Jersey Sweet Potato Chips (page 168)

2–4 lemon wedges, for garnish

1. In a large stainless steel bowl, mix the ground beef with the egg yolks, onion, parsley, anchovies, and capers. Mix in the mustard. Add the oil and mix until it is well incorporated. Season with salt and pepper.

2. Mold the tartare in the middle of a plate or platter and spread the chips all around. Garnish with additional chopped parsley and lemon wedges and serve.

Allen's Tip: **Steak tartare is not cooked, so choose the highest-quality beef you can find. Buy it from a reputable butcher who knows where the meat comes from and be sure it's fresh. Likewise, buy the freshest eggs you can find (or use pasteurized eggs).**

Tri-color Shoestring Fries with Nori "Salt" and Creamy Kimchi Dip

Lately I have been experimenting with Asian flavors and ingredients. In coming up with this recipe, I started off by doctoring up some kimchi I had on hand to make a creamy dip and figured that shoestring fries would pair perfectly with it. Nori, a type of seaweed, has an umami flavor that I use as a topping instead of traditional salt. (And did you know that seaweed has many beneficial nutritional properties?) If you want to add even more richness to this starter or snack, add a couple tablespoons of duck fat to the frying oil.

SERVES 4

1 sheet nori (dried seaweed)
1 teaspoon water
Sea salt, to taste
1 medium russet potato
1 medium sweet potato
1 medium Red Bliss potato

Rice bran or other neutral vegetable oil, for frying
Chopped scallions, for garnish
1 recipe Creamy Kimchi Dip (page 175), for serving

1. Preheat the oven to 375°F.

2. Place the nori on a rimmed baking sheet. Lightly sprinkle the water over the nori and give it a generous pinch of sea salt. Bake for about 5 minutes, or until the nori is crisp. Remove from the oven and let cool. Finely chop the nori and set it aside.

3. Using a mandoline or very sharp knife, cut the potatoes lengthwise into ⅛-inch-thick slices. Stack the slices and carefully cut them lengthwise again into ¼-inch-thick strips. Soak the shoestrings in a bowl of cold water for a few minutes and then pat them dry.

4. In a large saucepan, heat 3 inches of oil over medium heat until it shimmers and a deep-fry thermometer registers 375°F.

5. Working in batches so as not to crowd the pan, add a handful of shoestrings to the oil and fry for about 2 minutes, or until golden brown. Stir the shoestrings with tongs to prevent them from sticking together. Using a slotted spoon, transfer the shoestrings to paper towels to drain, and season with sea salt while hot. Allow the oil to regain temperature between batches.

6. Transfer the shoestrings to a serving dish and garnish with the chopped nori and scallions. Serve them with the dip on the side.

Reuben-Style Shoestring Cheese Fries

In Brooklyn, I grew up eating Reuben sandwiches—a classic with pastrami, sauerkraut, Swiss cheese, and tangy Russian dressing on rye bread. It's only natural that when experimenting with the menu at Potatopia, I came up with the idea to make a cheese-fry snack using the key elements from one of my favorite sandwiches. Here, I added some chiles to kick things up a notch, but the dish works just as well without them.

SERVES 2-4

2 tablespoons canola or corn oil
1 medium yellow onion, sliced
3 whole dried chiles de árbol (optional)
2 fresh thyme sprigs
2 bay leaves
1 clove garlic, minced
8 ounces sliced deli pastrami, chopped

1 recipe Shoestring Fries (page 169)
1 recipe Béchamel Sauce (page 175), hot, for serving
1 recipe Russian Dressing (page 176), for serving
Sliced scallions, for garnish

1. In a medium skillet, heat the oil over medium heat until it shimmers. Add the sliced onion and sauté for 5 minutes. Add the chiles (if using), thyme sprigs, bay leaves, and garlic and sauté for 5 minutes. Add the pastrami and sauté for 5 minutes. Remove the pan from the heat and discard the thyme, bay leaves, and chiles.

2. Put the fries on a serving plate. Pour the béchamel over the fries and top with the pastrami. Drizzle the dressing over all, garnish with scallions, and serve. If there are extra sauces, serve them on the side for dipping.

Potato and Goat Cheese Galette with Olives and Rosemary

I love this dish for its versatility. You can do so much when you start with a tender, flaky potato crust. I often add sausage, a wide range of cheeses, and other vegetables such as mushrooms and leeks to my galettes at home. In this recipe, crème fraîche and goat cheese help bond the herby filling, and they add some tang and creaminess to the dish.

SERVES 4–6

Dough

1¼ cups all-purpose flour
1¼ cups whole-wheat flour
1 tablespoon granulated sugar
¾ teaspoon salt
10 tablespoons cold unsalted butter, cut into ½-inch pieces
7 tablespoons ice water
1 teaspoon distilled white vinegar

Filling

1 pound Yukon Gold potatoes, peeled and rinsed
1 tablespoon olive oil
4–6 medium shallots, thinly sliced
1 teaspoon minced fresh rosemary
¼ cup crème fraîche
¼ cup chopped pitted Kalamata olives
1 teaspoon finely grated lemon zest
Salt and freshly ground black pepper, to taste

Assembly

2 teaspoons olive oil, divided
3 ounces goat cheese, crumbled
1 large egg, lightly beaten
Kosher salt
2 tablespoons minced fresh flat-leaf parsley

1. **For the dough:** Combine the all-purpose and whole-wheat flours, sugar, and salt in the bowl of a food processor. Pulse two or three times to combine. Add the butter and pulse until the mixture forms pea-size pieces, about 10 pulses. Transfer the flour-butter mixture to a bowl. Sprinkle the water and vinegar over the mixture. With a rubber spatula, use a folding motion to mix until the dry ingredients are moistened, but do not overwork the dough.

2. Transfer the dough to the center of a large sheet of plastic wrap. Press it gently into roughly a 4-inch square and wrap it tightly. Refrigerate for at least 45 minutes.

3. Transfer the dough to a lightly floured pastry cloth or countertop. Using a rolling pin, roll the dough into an 11 × 8-inch rectangle with the short sides parallel to the edge of the counter. Using a bench scraper or the pastry cloth, fold each short side in about 1½ inches and then bring the bottom third of the dough up and fold the top third over it, like a letter, into an 8 × 4-inch rectangle. Turn the dough 90 degrees counterclockwise and roll it out again into an 11 × 8-inch rectangle with the short sides still parallel to the counter. Fold it again into thirds. Turn the dough 90 degrees counterclockwise and repeat the rolling and folding process a third time. After the last fold, fold the dough in half to create a 4-inch square. Press the top of the dough gently. Wrap it in plastic wrap and refrigerate it for at least 45 minutes or up to 2 days.

4. **For the filling:** Using a mandoline or very sharp knife, cut the potatoes crosswise into ¼-inch-thick slices and place them in a microwave-safe bowl. Cover loosely with waxed paper and microwave on high power for 8 minutes, or until tender. Transfer the potato slices to a colander to drain and then return them to the bowl.

5. In a small skillet, heat the oil over medium heat until it shimmers. Add the shallots and rosemary, cover, and cook, stirring occasionally, until the shallots are tender and beginning to brown, about 5 minutes. Transfer the mixture to the bowl of potatoes. Stir in the crème fraîche, olives, and lemon zest. Season with salt and pepper and set aside.

6. **To assemble:** Remove the dough from the refrigerator and let it stand at room temperature for 15 to 20 minutes. Meanwhile, preheat the oven to 375°F. Set a rack in the middle position. Line a 14- to 16-inch round baking sheet with parchment paper.

7. On a generously floured work surface, roll out the dough to a 14-inch circle about ⅛ inch thick. Trim the edges as needed to form a circle. Transfer the circle of dough to the prepared baking sheet. With the tip of a paring knife, cut 5 small (¼-inch) holes in the dough: 1 in the center and 4 midway from the center, evenly spaced around the circle.

8. Brush the dough with 1 teaspoon of the oil. Spread half of the potato mixture evenly over the dough, leaving a 2-inch border around the edge. Sprinkle half of the goat cheese over the potato mixture, then top with the remaining potato mixture and goat cheese. Drizzle the remaining 1 teaspoon of oil over the filling. Gently grasp the edges of the dough and fold the outer 2 inches over the filling all around the galette, overlapping every 2 to 3 inches and gently pinching the pleated dough to secure it, but taking care not to press the dough into the filling. Brush the edges of the dough with the egg. Sprinkle kosher salt lightly all over the dough.

9. Place the galette in the oven and bake until the crust is deep golden brown and the filling is beginning to brown, 35 to 45 minutes. Transfer the pan to a wire rack to cool for 10 minutes. Using a wide metal spatula, loosen the galette from the parchment paper and carefully slide it onto a cutting board.

10. Sprinkle the galette with the parsley, cut it into wedges, and serve.

Potato Latkes with Creamed Caviar

This is a super tasty version of potato latkes. If you have never had them, latkes are potato pancakes eaten in Jewish households on holidays—and whenever you have extra potatoes on hand. My mother-in-law, who is also from Ukraine, likes to spread creamed caviar on toasted bread, but I had a feeling it would work even better on latkes. Some specialty supermarkets carry creamed caviar, but you might have more luck at an international supermarket or even online. In a pinch, you can mix a little salmon or other caviar with a touch of crème fraîche.

SERVES 4-6

Caviar Spread

1 (6.35-ounce) jar creamed caviar, such as Santa Bremor brand
2 tablespoons olive oil
¼ cup minced yellow onion
2 teaspoons distilled white or white wine vinegar

Latkes

3–4 medium russet potatoes, peeled and rinsed

½ cup grated sweet or yellow onion
2 large eggs, beaten
1 cup crushed sour cream and onion potato chips
2 teaspoons salt
1 teaspoon freshly ground black pepper
Rice bran or other neutral vegetable oil, for frying
Chopped fresh chives, for garnish

1. **For the caviar spread:** In a small bowl, combine all the ingredients and mix well. Refrigerate until ready to use.

2. **For the latkes:** Using the medium holes of a box grater, shred the potatoes into a bowl. Transfer the shredded potatoes to a clean kitchen towel. Gather the towel and squeeze the potatoes over the sink to remove any excess water. Return the shredded potatoes to the bowl. You should have about 3 cups.

3. In a large bowl, combine the shredded potatoes and onion and mix well. Add the eggs, chips, salt, and pepper and mix well.

4. In a large skillet, heat ¼ inch of oil over medium heat until it shimmers. Scoop out ⅓ cup of the potato mixture and use your hands to flatten the mixture into a patty. Working in batches, add the patties and cook, using a spatula to flatten them, for 3 to 5 minutes on each side, until the latkes are golden brown. You may need to adjust the heat so as not to burn them. Transfer the latkes to paper towels to drain. Repeat until all the potato mixture is used.

5. Transfer the warm latkes to a serving platter. Top each with a spoonful of the caviar cream. Garnish with chives and serve immediately.

Allen's Tip: **You can grate the potatoes by hand with a box grater, but if you have a food processor with a shredding attachment, that will save you time and effort.**

Potato, Corn, and Bacon Fritters

I came up with this craveable appetizer during a summer family cookout when I wanted to do something special with all the sweet corn I had on hand. I didn't want to serve plain corn on the cob. Instead, I blistered the corn on the grill and incorporated it into—what else? A potato dish that's sweet, crunchy, and savory all at the same time.

SERVES 4

1 large egg, separated
1¾ cups cooked fresh corn kernels or
    1 (15-ounce) can sweet corn, drained
½ cup all-purpose flour
¼ cup whole milk
1 cup leftover plain mashed potatoes

3 slices bacon, cooked crisp and crumbled
2 tablespoons chopped fresh thyme
8 tablespoons (1 stick) unsalted butter
2 tablespoons grated Parmesan
Chopped fresh chives, for garnish

1. Using a whisk, beat the egg white in a small bowl until stiff peaks form. Set aside.

2. In a medium bowl, combine the corn, flour, milk, and egg yolk. Stir just until the dry ingredients are moistened. Stir in the mashed potatoes, bacon, and thyme. Fold in the whipped egg white.

3. In a large nonstick skillet, melt the butter over medium heat until the foaming subsides. Working in batches, drop the potato mixture, one large spoonful at a time, into the butter and cook for about 3 minutes on each side, or until golden brown and crisp. Using a slotted spoon, transfer the fritters to paper towels to drain.

4. Transfer the fritters to a serving platter. Sprinkle the Parmesan and fresh chives over the fritters and serve.

Allen's Tip: **If you already have a grill going, shuck the corn and remove the silk. Grill the corn, turning occasionally, until the kernels are slightly charred and tender, about 10 minutes. (Alternatively, you can boil, steam, microwave, or roast the corn.) Allow to cool slightly, then stand each ear in a shallow dish and use a knife to slice off all the kernels.**

Skewered Grilled Potatoes with Herbed Yogurt Dip

My wife, Galina, always tries to find healthier ways to eat potatoes, especially for a cookout. This dish tastes great with any main course and pairs well with burgers, hot dogs, or grilled fish. The kids love it as well.

SERVES 4-6

10–12 small red potatoes
10–12 baby yellow potatoes
½ cup light mayonnaise
¼ cup dry white wine
2 teaspoons crushed dried rosemary
1 teaspoon garlic powder
½ teaspoon salt

½ teaspoon freshly ground black pepper
1 red bell pepper, seeded, membranes removed, and cut into 2-inch squares
1 yellow bell pepper, seeded, membranes removed, and cut into 2-inch squares
1 recipe Herbed Yogurt Dip (page 176), for serving

1. Put the potatoes in a large saucepan. Add enough cold salted water to cover them by 2 inches. Bring to a boil over high heat. Reduce the heat to medium and simmer for about 15 minutes, or until a sharp knife easily pierces the potatoes. Drain the potatoes and return them to the saucepan for a few minutes to dry.

2. In a large bowl, stir together the mayonnaise, wine, rosemary, garlic powder, salt, and pepper. Add the potatoes and bell peppers and toss to coat. Marinate the mixture, covered, in the refrigerator for 1 hour.

3. Meanwhile, soak 4 to 6 bamboo skewers in water for 30 minutes.

4. Preheat a gas or charcoal grill to high heat. Lightly oil the grate. Remove the potatoes from the marinade and reserve the marinade. Skewer the red and yellow potatoes alternately with the yellow and red bell peppers on the soaked bamboo skewers. Place on the grill and cook, covered, for 4 minutes. Brush the skewers with the reserved marinade and turn. Continue cooking for another 4 minutes.

5. Serve the skewers with the yogurt dip.

Sushi Tuna and Salmon Tartare Chips

As I mentioned earlier, I am a huge tartare fan. I also love sushi and potatoes, so why not combine all three passions? This light and delicious starter (or meal in itself) uses my Golden Potato Chips as the perfect base to showcase fresh salmon and tuna. Tobiko is flying fish roe. Many grocery stores sell it in small amounts, but you can also order a side of it at most sushi restaurants and counters.

MAKES 12 TARTARE CHIPS

6 tablespoons mayonnaise

1 tablespoon low-sodium soy sauce, plus more for dipping

1½ teaspoons hot pepper sauce

½ teaspoon rice vinegar

½ teaspoon wasabi powder

1 tablespoon tobiko

5 ounces sushi-grade raw salmon, chilled

5 ounces sushi-grade raw tuna, chilled

12 Golden Potato Chips (page 167) or store-bought thin waffle-style potato chips

Chopped fresh chives, for garnish

1. In a medium bowl, combine the mayonnaise, soy sauce, hot sauce, vinegar, wasabi powder, and tobiko and mix well.

2. Cut the salmon and tuna into ½-inch cubes. Add the fish to the mayonnaise mixture, gently folding it in until well combined.

3. Spoon about 1 tablespoon of the sushi mixture onto each chip. Place them on a serving platter and garnish with chives. Serve with a small bowl of soy sauce for dipping, if desired.

Golden Potato Skins with Creamy Portabella Mushroom Stuffing

As much as I love stuffed portabella mushrooms, for this recipe I wanted to flip the popular appetizer inside out. Instead of filling the mushroom cap with different fillings, here I make the potato the shell and fill it with savory, creamy mushrooms. Think of it as a new twist on potato skins.

SERVES 2–4

Potatoes

2 large Yukon Gold potatoes
2 tablespoons extra virgin olive oil
1 teaspoon kosher salt
1 teaspoon coarsely ground black pepper
1 teaspoon garlic powder
1 teaspoon dried basil

Mushroom Stuffing

¼ cup extra virgin olive oil
3 small shallots, minced
2 cloves garlic, minced
1½ tablespoons whole-grain mustard infused with Irish whiskey (available in gourmet shops and some supermarkets)

1 teaspoon fine sea salt
1 teaspoon coarsely ground black pepper
6 ounces portabella mushrooms, chopped
2 tablespoons dry white wine or vermouth
2 teaspoons chopped fresh flat-leaf parsley, plus more for garnish
¼ cup cream
1 tablespoon mascarpone cheese
2 tablespoons fresh breadcrumbs, divided
½ cup plus 2 tablespoons shredded Parmesan, divided
½ cup shredded smoked Gouda

1. Preheat the oven to 400°F. Grease a small baking pan.

2. **For the potatoes:** Put the potatoes in the prepared pan and bake for 40 to 50 minutes, until a sharp knife easily pierces the potatoes. Remove the potatoes from the oven and let cool for about 15 minutes. Keep the oven on.

3. Halve the potatoes lengthwise. Using a paring knife, cut around the edges of the potato halves ¼ inch from the edges. Scoop the centers of the potatoes into a bowl, leaving the shells intact, and set aside the flesh for another use.

4. In a small bowl, combine the oil, salt, pepper, garlic powder, and basil and mix well. Brush the insides and outsides of the potato shells with the oil mixture until coated. Transfer the oiled skins to a rimmed baking sheet and bake for 15 minutes, or until the edges brown and the skins begin to crisp.

5. **For the mushroom stuffing:** In a large skillet, heat the oil over medium heat until it shimmers. Add the shallots and garlic and sauté for 4 to 5 minutes, until translucent. Stir in the mustard, salt, and pepper. Continue to cook for about 1 minute, or until the seeds in the mustard start to pop. Add the mushrooms and cook for about 5 minutes, or until the mushrooms release their juices. Add the wine and cook until it reduces, about 1 minute. Add the parsley and cook for 2 minutes. Add the cream and bring to a simmer. Stir in the mascarpone cheese.

6. Preheat the broiler to high. In a large bowl, mix 1 tablespoon of the breadcrumbs with ¼ cup of the Parmesan. Add the hot mushroom filling to the bowl and stir until it's combined with the breadcrumb mixture. Spoon the filling into the potato shells.

7. In a small bowl, mix the remaining 1 tablespoon of breadcrumbs and another ¼ cup of the Parmesan. Stir in the Gouda. Spoon this topping onto the filled potatoes. Sprinkle the remaining 2 tablespoons of Parmesan over all.

8. Broil 4 to 5 inches from the heat source until the cheese is melted and the breadcrumbs are golden brown. Watch closely so as not to burn them. Transfer the potatoes to a platter, garnish with parsley, and serve.

Potato skins before and after broiling.

CHAPTER 2:
Soups and Salads

From the heartiest, most comforting bowl of soup to the lightest and bright- est salad, potatoes make a grand addition to a coursed meal or a quick and easy lunch or dinner.

67

Hearty Clam Chowder with Crispy Potato Skins

The year 2004 was a great one for me. Not only had I started my own media advertising company, but I also met my wife, Galina. I instantly fell in love with her beauty, fierce work ethic, and ambitious yet kind nature. Like mine, Galina's family emigrated here from Odessa, Ukraine, when she was just seven years old. She also started working at a very young age and was a dedicated student, later going on to work for Michael Bloomberg, former mayor of New York City. We married in 2005 and had two incredible sons, Landen in 2006 and Kyle in 2009. This is one of Galina's favorite soups. I love making this soup on a chilly, rainy Sunday afternoon while she is reading a book.

SERVES 2–3

2 tablespoons unsalted butter

1 medium Vidalia or other sweet onion, finely diced

2 celery ribs, quartered lengthwise and sliced crosswise into ¼-inch pieces

Salt and freshly ground black pepper, to taste

Red pepper flakes, to taste

3 tablespoons all-purpose flour

2 cups chicken or vegetable broth

2 (10-ounce) cans chopped clams, drained and juice reserved

1 cup heavy cream

2 bay leaves

3 medium russet potatoes, peeled (skins reserved) and cut into ½-inch cubes

½ cup canola oil

Chopped fresh flat-leaf parsley, for garnish

1. In a large saucepan, heat the butter over medium-high heat until the foaming subsides. Add the onion and celery and sauté for about 5 minutes, or until they are softened. Season with salt, black pepper, and red pepper flakes. Stir in the flour to distribute evenly. Add the broth, clam juice, cream, bay leaves, and potatoes and stir to combine. Bring the mixture to a simmer and cook, stirring constantly, until it thickens. Reduce the heat to medium-low and cook, stirring occasionally, for 20 minutes, or until the potatoes are tender.

2. Meanwhile, in a medium saucepan, heat the oil over medium heat until it shimmers. Add the potato peelings and cook for about 4 minutes, or until crisp. Transfer to paper towels to drain and season with salt, black pepper, and red pepper flakes while hot.

3. Once the potatoes are tender, stir in the clams and cook for another 2 minutes. Taste and add salt and black pepper as necessary. Remove the pan from the heat and discard the bay leaves.

4. Ladle the chowder into shallow bowls. Garnish with the crispy potato skins and parsley and serve.

Cream of Potato Soup with Porcini Mushrooms and Bacon

This creamy soup is my favorite to make on a cold winter day or when I just want a hearty, comforting meal. I like to use buttery yellow potatoes, sometimes called creamer potatoes, of which Yukon Gold is a popular variety. They tend to be wonderfully moist and just waxy enough to work beautifully in this recipe. When combined with butter, light cream, and lush mascarpone cheese, these spuds make for an indulgent, satisfying soup.

SERVES 4-6

½ ounce dried porcini mushrooms, sliced
4 tablespoons unsalted butter, divided
1 medium yellow onion, chopped
1½ celery ribs, thinly sliced
2 small carrots, peeled and thinly sliced
1 bay leaf
2 tablespoons chopped fresh flat-leaf parsley
1 teaspoon fine sea salt, divided, plus more to taste
1 teaspoon freshly ground black pepper, divided, plus more to taste
6 cloves garlic, divided

3 tablespoons all-purpose flour
2 cups chicken broth or stock
2 cups whole milk
2 tablespoons Worcestershire sauce
2 tablespoons dry white wine or vermouth
½ teaspoon cayenne pepper
4 medium Yukon Gold potatoes, cut into 2-inch cubes
2 tablespoons olive oil
1 fresh thyme sprig (optional)
4 slices thick-cut bacon
Microgreens, for garnish

1. Soak the mushrooms in a small bowl of room-temperature water for 30 minutes. Drain and rinse the mushrooms briefly to remove any sediment. Set them aside.

2. Preheat the oven to 375°F.

3. In a large saucepan, melt 3 tablespoons of the butter over medium heat until the foaming subsides. Add the onion, celery, carrots, bay leaf, and parsley. Season the mixture with ½ teaspoon each of the salt and black pepper. Lightly smash 3 of the garlic cloves with the flat part of a knife and add them to the saucepan. Cook for 3 minutes, then cover and continue cooking for about 5 more minutes, or until the vegetables have softened. Stir in the flour and cook for 1 minute. Stir in the broth, milk, Worcestershire sauce, wine, and cayenne pepper. Bring to a boil, reduce the heat to low, and simmer, stirring occasionally, for 15 to 20 minutes.

4. Meanwhile, in a large bowl, toss the potatoes with the olive oil and remaining ½ teaspoon each of the salt and black pepper. Transfer the potatoes to a rimmed baking sheet. Add the remaining 3 garlic cloves (whole) and the thyme sprig (if using). Bake for 10 minutes. While the potatoes are cooking, place the bacon slices in a single layer on a second rimmed baking sheet.

Recipe continues on next page

5. After 10 minutes, toss the potatoes. Return the baking sheet of potatoes to the oven, along with the baking sheet of bacon. Bake for 10 more minutes, or until a sharp knife easily pierces the potatoes and the bacon is crisp. Remove both baking sheets from the oven and transfer the bacon to paper towels to drain. When it is cool enough to handle, crumble into bite-size pieces.

6. Add the potatoes and garlic to the soup (discard the thyme, if using). Simmer until the potatoes are heated through, about 5 minutes. Remove and discard the bay leaf.

7. Meanwhile, in a skillet, melt the remaining 1 tablespoon of butter over medium heat until the foaming subsides. Add the mushrooms and sauté until they release their liquid and begin to caramelize, 6 to 8 minutes. Set aside.

8. Working in batches, carefully pour the soup into the bowl of a food processor and pulse to achieve the desired consistency, taking care not to process for too long or the soup will get too thick. (If you need to thin it, return it to the pot and whisk in a bit of water or milk.) Taste and add salt and pepper as necessary.

9. Ladle the soup into serving bowls. Garnish with the mushroom slices, crumbled bacon, and microgreens and serve.

Allen's Tip: **Yukon Gold potatoes do fine in a food processor, which makes quick work of this recipe. I would not use a food processor for whipped potatoes made with russets, for example, but for this recipe, it's the perfect device.**

Turnip, Maitake, and Potato Soup

While in San Francisco for a trip a while back, I ate a wonderful turnip and maitake mushroom soup. Maitakes, also known as hen of the woods, are delicious, richly flavored mushrooms. Back at home, of course I decided to add potatoes for even more substance and earthy flavor. The resulting soup has become a go-to for chillier days.

SERVES 6–8

4 tablespoons unsalted butter
2 medium yellow onions, thinly sliced
5 cloves garlic, minced
1 pound maitake mushrooms, sliced
1 pound young turnips, peeled and thinly sliced
5 large russet potatoes, peeled, rinsed, and thinly sliced
2 bay leaves

2 teaspoons salt, plus more to taste
1 teaspoon dried thyme
1 teaspoon dried sage
1 cup dry white wine
4 cups chicken broth or stock
Freshly ground black pepper, to taste
¼ teaspoon freshly grated nutmeg
2 tablespoons chopped fresh flat-leaf parsley, for garnish

1. In a large, heavy stockpot or Dutch oven, melt the butter over medium heat until the foaming subsides. Add the onions and garlic and cook until the onions are translucent but not browned, about 5 minutes. Add the maitakes and cook for another 2 to 3 minutes. Add the turnips and potatoes, stirring to coat with the butter. Stir in the bay leaves, salt, thyme, and sage. Cover and reduce the heat to low. Cook, stirring occasionally, for 20 minutes.

2. Add the wine and cook for 5 minutes. Add the chicken broth, raise the heat to high, and bring to a simmer. Reduce the heat to medium and cook, partially covered, until the turnips and potatoes are very tender, about 10 minutes. Remove and discard the bay leaves.

3. Working in batches, purée the soup in a blender until completely smooth. (When blending hot liquids, always remove the center cap from the blender lid and hold a kitchen towel firmly over the hole to allow steam to escape, or else the pressure can build inside and blow the lid off.) Return the soup to the pot and season with salt and pepper. Stir in the nutmeg. Ladle the soup into shallow bowls, garnish with the parsley, and serve.

Spiced Cream of Sweet Potato Soup

For this take on a fall soup, I like to season the potatoes with a little bacon-flavored dried molasses seasoning I found in the spice aisle of my grocery store, but if you can't find it and want to add a little smokiness, try a touch of smoked paprika instead.

SERVES 6

2 pounds sweet potatoes, peeled, rinsed, and cut into wedges

4 tablespoons olive oil, divided

1 teaspoon molasses-bacon seasoning, such as McCormick (optional)

1 head garlic

3 tablespoons unsalted butter

1 cup diced yellow onion

½ cup diced celery

½ cup peeled, diced carrot

⅛ teaspoon ground cinnamon

Pinch freshly grated nutmeg

Pinch ground allspice

1 bay leaf

4 cups chicken broth or stock

1 cup heavy cream

1 tablespoon dark brown sugar

½ teaspoon kosher salt

¼ teaspoon ground white pepper

6 tablespoons mascarpone cheese, for garnish

Chili powder, for garnish

1. Preheat the oven to 325°F.

2. In a bowl, toss the potatoes with 3 tablespoons of the olive oil and the molasses-bacon seasoning (if using) until lightly coated. Transfer to a rimmed baking sheet. Slice off the top portion of the head of garlic to expose the cloves and drizzle the remaining 1 tablespoon of olive oil over the exposed cloves to cover them. Wrap the garlic head in aluminum foil and place it on the baking sheet with the potatoes. Bake for 30 to 40 minutes, until the potato edges brown.

3. Squeeze the head of garlic from the sides to pop the softened roasted garlic cloves into a small bowl. Reserve 1½ teaspoons of the roasted garlic for this soup. Transfer the remaining roasted garlic to an airtight container and refrigerate for another use. It will keep for about 2 weeks.

4. In a heavy 3-quart saucepan, melt the butter over medium-high heat until the foaming subsides. Add the onion, celery, carrot, and reserved roasted garlic. Cook for 3 minutes, or until the vegetables are soft. Add the roasted potatoes, cinnamon, nutmeg, allspice, and bay leaf and stir continuously for 2 to 3 minutes, until the spices are aromatic.

5. Add the chicken broth, bring to a boil, reduce the heat to medium-low, and simmer for 30 minutes. Remove and discard the bay leaf.

6. In a small saucepan set over medium heat, warm the heavy cream, brown sugar, kosher salt, and white pepper, stirring frequently, for about 2 minutes. Slowly add the cream mixture to the soup while using an immersion blender to purée it directly in the pot. Alternatively, work in batches to purée the soup in a blender, pulsing until the soup is smooth. (When blending hot liquids, always remove the center cap from the blender lid and hold a kitchen towel firmly over the hole to allow steam to escape, or else the pressure can build inside and blow the lid off.)

7. Divide the soup evenly among 6 bowls. Garnish each serving with 1 tablespoon of the mascarpone and a pinch of chili powder. Serve hot.

French Onion Soup with Crispy Potato Galettes

French onion soup is my favorite soup of all time. I fell in love with it not in Paris, but at a French restaurant in Las Vegas where my parents took my brother, sister, and me when I was 11. When preparing ideas for this book, I knew I would want to include a version of this soup but swap out the bread for potatoes. Potato galettes are also classic French fare, and it turns out that they pair beautifully with French onion soup.

SERVES 4

8 tablespoons (1 stick) unsalted butter
4 yellow onions, chopped or sliced
2 cloves garlic, minced
2 bay leaves
1 bunch fresh thyme sprigs
Salt and freshly ground black pepper, to taste
2 cups dry red wine
2 heaping tablespoons all-purpose flour (optional)

6 cups beef broth or stock
1 teaspoon toasted mustard seeds, or to taste
4 (6-inch) Crispy Potato Galettes, warm (page 148; see Allen's Tip)
8 ounces Gruyère, shredded
Chopped fresh chives, for garnish

1. In a large saucepan, melt the butter over medium heat until the foaming subsides. Add the onions, garlic, bay leaves, thyme sprigs, salt, and pepper. Cook, stirring frequently, until the onions are very soft and caramelized, about 25 minutes. Add the wine and bring to a boil. Reduce the heat to medium-low and simmer until the wine has evaporated and the onions are dry, about 5 minutes. Remove and discard the bay leaves and thyme.

2. For a thicker soup, add the flour to the onions and cook for 10 minutes to cook out the raw flour taste.

3. Add the beef broth, bring the soup to a simmer, and cook for 10 minutes. Add the mustard seeds and season with salt and pepper.

4. Preheat the broiler.

5. Ladle the soup into 4 (6-inch) oven-safe bowls. Top each with a potato galette. Sprinkle the cheese over the galettes. Broil until bubbly and golden brown, 3 to 5 minutes. Garnish with fresh chives and serve.

Roasted Potato and Sweet Corn Chowder

I am not usually a fan of chunky soups, but New Jersey had a massive blizzard one day, and we were hit with record snowfall. As my family and I were home all day, my wife said to me, "I would love a hearty corn chowder on a day like today." Most potato and corn chowders call for plain, sautéed potatoes, but I always prefer to season and roast the potatoes to add more flavor and texture to this soup, which we now eat all year long.

SERVES 4–6

7–9 small red potatoes, diced (about 3 cups)
2 tablespoons olive oil
3 cloves garlic, lightly smashed
½ teaspoon salt, plus more to taste
½ teaspoon freshly ground black pepper, plus more to taste
4 cups fresh sweet corn kernels, or 2 (15-ounce) cans sweet corn, drained
2 tablespoons pure maple syrup
2 tablespoons unsalted butter
1 cup chopped celery
1 cup chopped yellow onion
3 canned chipotles in adobo sauce, chopped
3 tablespoons all-purpose flour
3½ cups chicken broth or stock
2 cups whole milk
2 cups shredded smoked Gouda
Microgreens, for garnish

1. Preheat the oven to 375°F.

2. In a bowl, toss the potatoes with the olive oil, garlic, salt, and pepper. Transfer to a rimmed baking sheet. Bake for 30 to 40 minutes, turning and tossing about halfway through, until the potatoes are golden brown and crunchy.

3. When the potatoes are about halfway done, in a separate bowl combine the corn, maple syrup, and a pinch each of salt and pepper and mix well. Transfer to a second rimmed baking sheet and place in the oven, on a separate rack from the potatoes, and bake for 15 to 20 minutes, until the corn starts to brown slightly. Remove both baking sheets from the oven and set aside.

4. In large saucepan, melt the butter over medium-high heat until the foaming subsides. Add the celery and onion and sauté until tender, about 5 minutes. Stir in the chipotles and flour and stir to blend well. Add the chicken broth and bring to a boil. Reduce the heat to medium-low and simmer for 8 to 10 minutes.

5. Reserve about a quarter of the potatoes and corn for the garnish. Stir the remaining potatoes and corn into the soup. Stir in the milk and bring it back to a simmer, stirring often, for about 5 minutes. Reduce the heat to low and stir in the Gouda, stirring until it melts completely. Taste and add salt and pepper as necessary.

6. Ladle the soup into shallow bowls. Garnish with the reserved potatoes, corn, and microgreens and serve.

Red Bliss Potato Salad with Tangy Pepper Sauce and Manchego

Manchego is a Spanish cheese that has a wonderfully nutty flavor. It pairs well with the mild, sweet Spanish Padrón chile used in my Tangy Pepper Sauce. You should be able to find these chiles at your local grocer, but if not, look for the shishito (a close cousin) at an Asian market. Think of this dish as a more colorful, Spanish-inspired potato salad; the chiles, when roasted first, give the creamy dressing a smoky richness.

SERVES 4–6

10 baby Red Bliss potatoes (about 1 pound), quartered
1 recipe Tangy Pepper Sauce (page 176)
¾ cup shredded Manchego
Salt, to taste
Chopped fresh chives, for garnish

1. Put the potatoes in a large saucepan and add enough cold salted water to cover them by 2 inches. Bring to a boil over high heat. Reduce the heat to medium and simmer for about 20 minutes, or until a sharp knife easily pierces the potatoes. Drain the potatoes in a colander and set aside to cool a bit.

2. Transfer the potatoes to a large bowl. Add the sauce, Manchego, and salt and toss until well combined. Cover and refrigerate for at least 30 minutes or up to 8 hours.

3. Garnish with chives and serve.

Roasted Baby Dutch Potato and Smoked Salmon Salad

I love smoked salmon (also called lox) on bagels with cream cheese. In my family, a traditional breakfast would include that but also some boiled potatoes with garlic and dill, and a little bit of raw onion. In this recipe, I've swapped the bagel and cream cheese for a potato salad that becomes a delicious base for the lox.

SERVES 4–6

25 baby Yellow Dutch potatoes
2 tablespoons olive oil
4 cloves garlic, minced
½ teaspoon fine sea salt, plus a pinch
½ teaspoon coarsely ground black pepper,
    plus a pinch
Juice of 1 lemon, divided
½ cup cream cheese

¼ cup crème fraîche
½ small yellow onion
1 small bunch fresh dill, stemmed and
    chopped, divided
2 ounces smoked salmon, chopped
1 large egg yolk, hard cooked and
    crumbled, divided

1. Preheat the oven to 375°F.

2. In a medium bowl, combine the potatoes, olive oil, garlic, salt, and pepper and mix well. Transfer to a rimmed baking sheet and bake for 20 minutes, or until a sharp knife easily pierces the potatoes.

3. In a bowl, toss the potatoes with 2 teaspoons of the lemon juice and let stand for 10 minutes. Transfer, uncovered, to the refrigerator and chill for 30 minutes.

4. Halve the potatoes lengthwise. Some parts of the skin might peel away; that's okay.

5. In a large bowl, whisk together the cream cheese, crème fraîche, yellow onion, three-quarters of the dill, the remaining lemon juice, and a pinch each of salt and pepper. Fold in the potatoes, smoked salmon, and half of the egg yolk crumbles. Gently mix until combined.

6. Garnish with the remaining egg crumbles and dill and serve.

Roasted Sweet Potato, Hazelnut, and Apple Salad

One day I was in the mood for a light, fresh salad for lunch. I had hazelnuts on hand, along with some apples and sweet potatoes, and I decided to combine them all. You'll see I added my trusty bacon-flavored molasses spice (available at any grocery store) as a seasoning for the potatoes, but if you can't find it, you can omit it or try smoked paprika instead. Better yet, add your own bacon bits if you have them on hand. In the style of a classic Waldorf salad, I made a creamy dressing using my Ranch Dip recipe and kicked things up a notch heatwise with a touch of pepperoncini juice.

SERVES 2-4

1 large sweet potato, peeled, rinsed, and cut into 2-inch cubes
3–4 tablespoons extra virgin olive oil
3 tablespoons molasses-bacon seasoning, such as McCormick (optional)
Generous pinch kosher salt

¾ cup toasted hazelnuts
1 small red apple
1 small cucumber
⅓ cup Ranch Dip (page 174)
1½ teaspoons liquid from bottled hot pepperoncini peppers

1. Preheat the oven to 400°F.

2. In a medium bowl, toss the sweet potato with the oil. Add the molasses-bacon seasoning (if using) and salt and toss well. Transfer the potato mixture to a rimmed baking sheet and bake for 15 to 18 minutes, until the edges of the sweet potato cubes are golden brown. Transfer to a large bowl, cover, and refrigerate for at least 30 minutes.

3. Meanwhile, in a large sauté pan, toast the hazelnuts over medium-high heat, swirling the pan to prevent burning, for 2 to 3 minutes, until fragrant and beginning to brown. Remove the hazelnuts from the pan, let cool, and coarsely chop them.

4. Using a mandoline or sharp knife, thinly slice the apple and cucumber. Add them to the bowl with the sweet potato. In a separate bowl, whisk together the dip and pepperoncini liquid. Add it to the salad and toss well.

5. Garnish the salad with the hazelnuts and serve.

Potato, Arugula, Pesto, and Prosciutto Salad

Pesto goes great with pasta, of course, but it's also delicious with potatoes. Try this Italian-inspired twist on a potato salad with some extra green from fresh, seasonal arugula and a little savory addition from the prosciutto.

SERVES 2

1 medium russet potato, peeled and rinsed

1 cup packed fresh arugula

3–4 tablespoons Allen's Pesto (page 177)

2 tablespoons grated Parmesan

2 tablespoons toasted pine nuts

4 slices prosciutto di Parma

Freshly ground black pepper, to taste

1. Put the potato in a medium saucepan and add enough cold salted water to cover it by 2 inches. Bring to a boil over high heat. Reduce the heat to medium and simmer for 15 to 20 minutes, until a sharp knife easily pierces the potato. Drain the potato in a colander for 10 minutes. Transfer it to the refrigerator to cool completely, about 1 hour.

2. Cut the potato into 1-inch cubes. Put the potato cubes in a serving bowl and add the arugula, pesto, Parmesan, and pine nuts. Mix well.

3. Divide the salad between 2 serving plates. Place the prosciutto slices atop or around the salad. Season with a few grinds of pepper and serve.

Spicy Edamame Potato Salad

This dish came about from a failed creation of another Asian-style dish that included eda-mame and was meant to be served hot. I liked the flavor profile, but the texture didn't work. The next time, I recreated it in cold form and it turned out delicious.

SERVES 4–6

1 pound frozen edamame
14–18 small red potatoes (about 2 pounds)
Juice of 1 lime
3 tablespoons olive oil
1 tablespoon toasted sesame oil
1 teaspoon minced garlic

¼ teaspoon minced fresh ginger
1 teaspoon hot mustard powder
½ teaspoon red pepper flakes
2 scallions, thinly sliced
Kosher salt and freshly ground black
    pepper, to taste

1. Bring a large saucepan of salted water to a boil over high heat. Add the edamame and cook for 1 to 2 minutes, until thawed and crisp-tender. Using a slotted spoon, trans-fer the edamame to a bowl of ice water, leaving the cooking water in the saucepan.

2. Add the potatoes to the saucepan, making sure the water covers the potatoes by at least 1 inch; add more water if it doesn't. Bring to a boil over high heat. Reduce the heat to medium and simmer for about 15 minutes, or until a sharp knife easily pierces the potatoes. Drain the potatoes and transfer them to a bowl of ice water. When the potatoes are just cool enough to handle, drain them in a colander.

3. While the potatoes cool, in a large bowl, whisk together the lime juice, olive and sesame oils, garlic, ginger, hot mustard powder, and red pepper flakes.

4. When the potatoes have drained, quarter them and add them to the bowl. Toss well and add the scallions. Toss again and season with salt and pepper. Refrigerate, cov-ered, for at least 1 hour and serve chilled.

CHAPTER 3:
Mains

For so long, potatoes have been thought of only as a side dish or snack, but in this book—and particularly in this chapter—I make potatoes the main attraction. Here you will find new takes on old favorites, showcasing the potato in all its glory. In some cases, I have chosen to pair potatoes with meat or fish, but in each instance, I've tried to create something unique and wonderful, a shining-star component that goes beyond your typical "supporting role" potato dishes.

Pictured, clockwise from top: Herb-Crusted Lamb Chops with Crispy Potato Wedges (p. 94); Cheesy Red Potato Casserole with Croutons and Chives (p. 138); Layered Mashed Potato and Truffled Mushroom Casserole (p. 133)

Chicken Milanese with Mascarpone Sauce and Baby Dutch Crispy Potatoes

One of my favorite dishes in Italian restaurants is veal Milanese with arugula salad on top. My kids, however, prefer a chicken cutlet instead of veal. So I used that as the inspiration for this twist on the classic and incorporated crispy potatoes instead of the bowl of pasta you might normally get. My two boys eat chicken cutlets at least three times a week after school or for dinner. They said this was the best chicken cutlet they ever tried!

SERVES 4–6

⅓ cup seasoned dry breadcrumbs
¼ cup canned French-fried onions, such as French's
¼ cup grated Parmesan
2 large eggs
¼ cup all-purpose flour
6 (4-ounce) boneless, skinless chicken breasts
Salt and freshly ground black pepper, to taste
20–25 baby Yellow Dutch potatoes (about 1 pound)

1½ cups canola oil, divided
1 tablespoon olive oil
½ small yellow onion, minced
10 cherry tomatoes
2 cloves garlic, minced
1 teaspoon dried thyme
½ teaspoon red pepper flakes
½ cup mascarpone cheese
1 tablespoon sliced fresh basil

1. In the bowl of a food processor, combine the breadcrumbs, fried onions, and Parmesan. Pulse until finely chopped, then transfer the breadcrumb mixture to a large shallow bowl. In a second large shallow bowl, beat the eggs. Put the flour in a third large shallow bowl.

2. On a clean work surface, place the chicken between 2 large pieces of plastic wrap. Using a meat mallet, lightly pound the chicken to a ¼- to ½-inch thickness. Season the chicken with salt and pepper.

3. Place 1 chicken breast in the flour, turning to coat both sides lightly. Dip the floured chicken into the beaten eggs, turning to coat both sides, and let the excess egg drip back into the bowl. Place the chicken in the breadcrumb mixture, pressing gently and flipping to coat both sides. Transfer the chicken to a rimmed baking sheet. Repeat the process with the remaining chicken, arranging the breaded cutlets on top of each other on the baking sheet. Refrigerate the chicken while you prepare the potatoes.

4. Preheat the oven to 150°F.

5. Put the potatoes in a large saucepan and add enough cold salted water to cover them by 2 inches. Bring to a boil over high heat. Reduce the heat to medium and simmer for about 15 minutes, or until a sharp knife easily pierces the potatoes. Drain the potatoes in a colander and set aside to cool. When the potatoes are cool enough to handle, halve them lengthwise.

The Potatopia Cookbook

6. Pour 1 cup of the canola oil into a large nonstick sauté pan and heat over medium heat until it shimmers. Working in batches so as not to crowd the pan, add a handful of potatoes to the oil and fry for about 5 minutes, or until the potatoes are crisp on the outside and soft inside. Stir the potatoes with tongs to prevent them from sticking together. Using a slotted spoon, transfer the potatoes to a rimmed baking sheet. Season with salt while hot and place the baking sheet in the oven to keep the potatoes warm. Allow the oil to regain temperature between batches.

7. In a large nonstick sauté pan, heat the remaining ½ cup of canola oil over medium heat until it shimmers. Add 3 of the chicken cutlets and cook for 3 to 4 minutes on each side, until golden brown. Transfer the chicken to the baking sheet with the potatoes in the oven to keep warm. Repeat with the remaining 3 chicken cutlets. Reserve the cooking juices in the sauté pan.

8. Add the olive oil to the reserved cooking juices and heat over medium heat until it shimmers. Add the onion and cook, stirring frequently, until softened, 4 to 5 minutes. Stir in the cherry tomatoes, garlic, thyme, red pepper flakes, salt, and pepper. Cook for 5 to 6 minutes, until the tomatoes are tender. Remove the pan from the heat. Add the mascarpone cheese and basil and stir until the cheese is melted and the sauce is creamy.

9. Transfer the chicken to a serving platter and spoon the potatoes on top. Pour the sauce over the potatoes and serve immediately.

"Hangover" Breakfast Perfection

Growing up, my father would make what I now call his "hangover" morning meal of hash browns, sausage, cheddar, and chives for breakfast. As an adult, I enjoy this after a late night with friends or when I'm just hungry for a filling, hearty weekend brunch.

SERVES 1–2

1 medium russet potato, peeled and rinsed

1 tablespoon unsalted butter, plus more as needed

½ stick Kowalski Hunter's Sausage or other dried sausage stick, cut into ¾-inch strips

2 cloves garlic, minced

3 large eggs

Salt and freshly ground black pepper, to taste

Shredded cheddar or American cheese (optional)

Chopped fresh chives, for garnish

1. Using a mandoline or very sharp knife, cut the potato lengthwise into ⅛-inch-thick slices. Stack the slices and carefully cut them lengthwise again into ¼-inch-thick shoestrings. Soak the shoestrings in a bowl of cold water for a few minutes and then pat them dry with paper towels.

2. In a large nonstick skillet, melt the butter over medium heat until the foaming subsides. Add the sausage and cook for about 5 minutes, or until the sausage is crisp but not too brown. Transfer to a paper towel to drain.

3. Add the shoestrings to the skillet and cook until they start to brown, about 7 minutes. (Add more butter, if necessary; the pan should not smoke.) Stir in the garlic and cook for 1 minute. Return the sausage to the skillet and stir well. Crack the eggs over the shoestrings. Cover and cook until the egg whites are set, about 3 minutes. Season with salt and pepper.

4. Top with cheese, if desired. Garnish with chopped chives and serve.

Hash Brown Eggs Benedict with Tuscan Ham

Eggs Benedict is a favorite of mine when we go out for brunch. Sometimes it's served with hash browns on the side, but I wanted to try moving the hash browns to the center of the plate in place of the English muffin. So I did just that, and when paired with Tuscan ham instead of the traditional Canadian bacon, the dish was a little more elevated and a lot more delicious. Even better, the hash browns helped soak up all that delicious sauce from the egg yolks and the hollandaise.

SERVES 2

1 medium russet potato, peeled and rinsed
2 tablespoons unsalted butter, melted
1 large egg yolk
Pinch salt, plus more to taste
Pinch freshly ground black pepper
Pinch cayenne pepper, plus more for garnish

2 tablespoons shredded Pecorino Romano (optional)
3 tablespoons extra virgin olive oil, divided
6–8 slices deli Tuscan ham or Romano ham
1 tablespoon white wine vinegar
4 large eggs
1 recipe Hollandaise Sauce (page 174), warm

1. Using the medium holes of a box grater, shred the potato into a bowl of cold water. Drain the potato and transfer it to a clean kitchen towel. Gather the towel and squeeze the potato over the sink to remove any excess water. Transfer the shredded potato to a medium bowl.

2. Add the melted butter, egg yolk, salt, black pepper, and cayenne pepper and mix well. Mix in the Pecorino (if using). Divide the potato mixture in half and shape each half into an oval patty.

3. In a small skillet, heat 2 tablespoons of the oil over medium heat until it shimmers. Add the potato patties and cook for about 4 minutes per side, or until golden brown. Transfer the hash brown patties to paper towels to drain.

4. In the same skillet, heat the remaining 1 tablespoon of oil over medium heat until it shimmers. Add the ham and cook for about 30 seconds on each side, or until it's just crisp. Transfer the ham to a paper towel to drain.

5. Fill a medium saucepan with water and bring to a boil over high heat. Reduce the heat to medium and maintain a gentle simmer—you do not want a vigorous boil. Add the vinegar and a pinch of salt. Crack the eggs, one at a time, into 4 small dishes.

6. Whisk the boiling water to create a vortex in the center. Gently slide 1 egg into the vortex and cook for 30 to 45 seconds, until the white is set. (Cook longer for less runny eggs.) Using a slotted spoon, gently transfer the egg to a colander to drain. Repeat this process with the remaining eggs.

7. Place the hash brown patties in the center of each of 2 warm serving plates. Top with the crispy ham slices and 2 poached eggs per patty. Pour the hollandaise sauce over the eggs and garnish with a pinch of cayenne. Serve right away.

Hearty Shepherd's Pie with Tangy Pepper Sauce

A while back I was invited to do a TV demo for St. Patrick's Day and to promote Potatopia. In thinking about what potato dish I could do, I came up with a classic shepherd's pie, but I served it with a side that used a green sauce inspired by the Irish holiday. This is the same green-tinted pepper sauce I use with my Red Bliss Potato Salad (page 77).

SERVES 6

Potatoes

3 medium russet potatoes, peeled and rinsed
2 teaspoons kosher salt
¾ cup shredded Parmesan
1 tablespoon chopped fresh rosemary
2 teaspoons unsalted butter, melted
Freshly ground black pepper, to taste

Filling

2 tablespoons olive oil
1 medium yellow onion, minced
2 medium carrots, peeled and minced
3 cloves garlic, minced

12 ounces ground veal or lamb
12 ounces ground beef
¼ teaspoon salt
¼ teaspoon freshly ground black pepper
2 tablespoons all-purpose flour
2 tablespoons tomato paste
1 cup chicken broth or stock
½ cup frozen corn kernels
2 tablespoons Worcestershire sauce
2 teaspoons liquid smoke or smoked paprika (optional)
1 tablespoon chopped fresh thyme
1 recipe Tangy Pepper Sauce (page 176)

1. **For the potatoes:** Using the medium holes of a box grater, shred the potatoes into a large saucepan of cold water. The water should cover the potatoes by about 1 inch; add more if necessary. Add the salt and bring to a boil over high heat. Reduce the heat to medium and simmer 8 to 10 minutes, until the potatoes are tender.

2. Drain the potatoes in a colander and rinse them with cold water. Transfer them to a clean kitchen towel. Gather the towel and gently squeeze the potatoes over the sink to remove any excess water. Transfer the potatoes to a medium bowl. Add the Parmesan, rosemary, and butter and mix well. Season with a few grinds of black pepper and set aside.

3. Preheat the oven to 400°F.

4. **For the filling:** In a 12-inch skillet, heat the oil over medium heat until it shimmers. Add the onion and carrots and sauté for 5 minutes, or until the onion has softened. Add the garlic and sauté for 1 minute. Add the veal, beef, salt, and pepper and sauté, stirring to break up the meat, until it is no longer pink, 5 to 7 minutes. Stir in the flour and mix well. Stir in the tomato paste and cook for 1 minute. Add the chicken broth, corn, Worcestershire sauce, liquid smoke or smoked paprika (if using), and thyme and mix well. Bring to a simmer and cook for 1 to 2 minutes.

5. Transfer the hot filling to a shallow 1½-quart casserole dish. Spread the potato mixture evenly over the filling.

6. Bake the pie for 10 to 15 minutes, until heated through. Raise the oven temperature to 500°F or turn on the broiler. Broil the pie 4 to 5 inches from the heat source for 10 minutes, or until the top is nicely browned and crisp.

7. Cut the pie into wedges and serve with the pepper sauce on the side or drizzled over the top.

Herb-Crusted Lamb Chops with Crispy Potato Wedges

About three years ago I had an herb-crusted crispy lamb chop at a French restaurant in San Diego that was better than anything I had ever tasted. I knew I had to find a way to recreate it at home—and of course to incorporate some crispy potato wedges into the dish. The secret to this dish's success is to have your butcher "french" the rib bones, which means to scrape them clean of any meat. You can also try this yourself: hold the end of each rib bone and use a sharp knife to scrape back any residual meat so the bone is exposed.

SERVES 4

3 medium russet potatoes, cut lengthwise
    into 12 wedges each and rinsed
5–6 tablespoons olive oil, divided
½ cup plain or seasoned dry breadcrumbs
1 tablespoon granulated garlic
2 teaspoons chopped fresh chives
1 teaspoon coarse sea salt
1 teaspoon ground white pepper
½ teaspoon chopped fresh rosemary
1 (8-rib) rack of lamb, frenched

Kosher salt and freshly ground black
    pepper, to taste
2 cloves garlic, minced
¼ cup chopped fresh flat-leaf parsley
1 tablespoon chopped fresh thyme
1 cup soft fresh breadcrumbs, preferably
    from French bread
2 tablespoons Dijon mustard or spicy
    brown mustard

1. Preheat the oven to 400°F. Grease a rimmed baking sheet.

2. In a large bowl, combine the potato wedges and 2 tablespoons of the oil and toss to coat well. In a small bowl, combine the dry breadcrumbs, granulated garlic, chives, sea salt, white pepper, and rosemary and mix well. Add the breadcrumb mixture to the potatoes and toss to coat well. Transfer the potatoes to the prepared baking sheet and bake for 20 minutes.

3. While the potatoes bake, season the lamb with kosher salt and black pepper. Combine the minced garlic, parsley, thyme, and soft breadcrumbs in a shallow dish or pie plate. Moisten the mixture with enough of the remaining 3 to 4 tablespoons of olive oil to make the mixture hold together. Set the herbed breadcrumb mixture aside.

4. Heat a large skillet over high heat. Place the lamb, meaty side down, in the skillet. Using tongs, hold the lamb against the dry skillet for 1 minute to give it a nice brown crust. Turn the meat to sear it on all sides for 1 minute each. Transfer the meat to a cutting board and carefully spread the mustard over the entire rack. Roll the meat in the herbed breadcrumb mixture to coat it. Use your hands to spread the rest of the mixture over the top, patting to coat it evenly.

5. Cover the exposed rib bones with strips of aluminum foil so they do not burn. Place the rack on a rimmed baking sheet. Transfer to the oven with the potatoes, raise the temperature to 475°F, and roast both the lamb and potatoes for 18 to 20 minutes, until an instant-read thermometer inserted into the thickest part of the meat registers 145°F for medium rare. Keep a close eye on the potatoes; remove them when they are crisp and golden brown.

6. After the potatoes are removed, turn on the broiler and broil the lamb for 1 to 2 minutes to get a crispier crust, if desired. When the lamb comes out of the oven, turn off the oven and return the potatoes to keep warm while finishing the lamb.

7. Let the lamb rest for about 2 minutes. To carve, remove the foil strips and cut the rack into 4 (2-rib) sections. Pile the roasted potatoes in the center of each of 4 plates. Place a 2-rib section of lamb on top and serve.

Japanese Yams with Marinated Bulgogi

Japanese yams—with their purple skin and yellow flesh—are by far my favorite type of yam because of their mildly sweet taste after roasting. They are mainly sold in Asian markets; if you can't find them, it's okay to use a regular sweet potato in this recipe. I decided to pair the yams with bulgogi, or Korean barbecued beef, which I always order at Korean restaurants and love for its flavor-packed marinade. Once in a while, I'll season the yams with a little umami-rich MSG, but sea salt is just fine, too.

SERVES 2-4

⅓ cup soy sauce

¼ cup sliced scallions, plus more for garnish

2½ tablespoons granulated sugar

2 tablespoons white sesame seeds

2 tablespoons toasted sesame oil

2 tablespoons minced garlic

1 teaspoon grated fresh ginger

½ teaspoon freshly ground black pepper

¾–1 pound boneless beef rib-eye or top sirloin steak, very thinly sliced (see Allen's Tip)

2 jumbo Japanese yams (6–8 ounces each)

Olive oil, for searing

1 tablespoon unsalted butter

Umami seasoning (MSG) or sea salt, to taste

1. Preheat the oven to 375°F.

2. In a shallow bowl, whisk together the soy sauce, scallions, sugar, sesame seeds, sesame oil, garlic, ginger, and pepper. Add the beef and use your hands to mix and coat the meat. Cover and refrigerate for at least 1 hour to marinate.

3. While the beef is marinating, put the yams on a rimmed baking sheet and bake for about 1 hour, or until a sharp knife easily pierces the yams. Turn off the oven, but keep the yams inside to keep warm until the beef is cooked.

4. Lightly coat a stovetop griddle or large skillet with olive oil and heat it over medium-high heat. Working in batches so as not to crowd the pan, use tongs to place the slices of beef on the griddle. Cook for about 1 minute on each side, or until browned. Transfer to a plate.

5. Cut the yams lengthwise and lightly fluff the insides with a fork, as you would for a regular baked potato. Add the butter and umami seasoning (if using) and mix lightly with the fork. Add the cooked beef, garnish with scallions, and serve.

Allen's Tip: **Bulgogi traditionally uses very thinly sliced high-quality steaks, so ask your butcher to slice the meat for you, or try it yourself by freezing the meat for a few minutes to firm it up and then using a very sharp knife (and some extra care and attention) to slice it thin.**

Potato Lasagna Bolognese

I have always loved lasagna for its big, bold flavors and textures. One day, while admiring all those delicious lasagna layers at a restaurant, I thought, *Why not layer a lasagna with potato slices instead of pasta?* This hearty, gluten-free casserole really does feed and please a crowd. Be sure to slice the potatoes as thin as possible using a sharp knife or mandoline; otherwise the lasagna will be too heavy.

SERVES 8–10

Potatoes

5–6 medium russet potatoes, peeled and rinsed

Bolognese Sauce

¼ cup olive oil
1 medium yellow onion, finely chopped
1 large carrot, finely chopped
1 celery rib, finely chopped
2–3 cloves garlic, minced
¼ cup tomato paste
1½ pounds ground beef
1½ pounds ground veal
1 cup dry white wine
½ cup whole milk

¼ cup finely chopped and strained fresh tomatoes
1½ teaspoons dried thyme
Salt and freshly ground black pepper, to taste

Filling

5 cups whole-milk ricotta
¾ cup whole milk
4 large eggs, lightly beaten
1 cup grated Parmesan, divided
½ teaspoon freshly grated or ground nutmeg
Salt and freshly ground black pepper
Fresh basil leaves, for garnish

1. **For the potatoes:** Put the potatoes in a large saucepan and add enough cold salted water to cover them by 2 inches. Bring to a boil over high heat. Reduce the heat to medium and simmer for 5 to 7 minutes, until the potatoes are tender enough to slice easily but are not cooked through. Drain the potatoes and let them stand until they are cool enough to handle.

2. Using a mandoline or very sharp knife, cut the potatoes lengthwise into very thin strips, submerging them in a large bowl of cold water as you go to prevent browning. Each slice should be as thin as a potato chip, or as close as you can make it. Set the potatoes aside.

3. **For the Bolognese sauce:** In a 12- to 14-inch heavy skillet or sauté pan, heat the oil over medium heat until it shimmers. Add the onion, carrot, celery, garlic, and tomato paste and cook, stirring occasionally, for 12 to 15 minutes, until the vegetables are golden and softened. Add the beef and veal and cook, stirring to break up the meat, for 7 to 8 minutes, until the meat is mostly no longer pink. Add the wine and cook for 8 to 10 minutes, until the wine evaporates and the meat is uniformly browned.

4. Add the milk, strained tomatoes, and thyme. Reduce the heat to medium-low and simmer gently, stirring occasionally, for about 1 hour, or until the liquid evaporates but the mixture is still moist. Taste and season the sauce with salt and pepper. Remove the pan from the heat and set aside.

Recipe continues on next page

5. **For the filling:** Whisk together the ricotta, milk, eggs, ½ cup of the Parmesan, and the nutmeg. Season with salt and pepper. Set the filling aside.

6. Preheat the oven to 375°F. Grease a deep 13 × 9-inch baking dish.

7. Drain the potato slices and pat dry with paper towels. Transfer them to kitchen towels and let them dry completely. The slices should be as dry as possible.

8. Spread some of the potatoes across the bottom of the prepared dish. They should mostly be in a single layer, but there can be a little overlap. Sprinkle with some of the remaining ½ cup of Parmesan. Spread about 1½ cups of the Bolognese sauce over the Parmesan and then top with a layer of the filling. Repeat this process to make three or four layers, ending with a final layer of the potatoes and a sprinkling of the Parmesan.

9. Bake for about 30 minutes, or until a sharp knife easily pierces the potatoes on top, the top is crispy and brown, and the filling is bubbling around the sides of the dish.

10. Let the lasagna stand for 5 minutes before cutting. Garnish with basil and serve.

Layering the potatoes.

Maple-Glazed Salmon with Baby Purple Potatoes

Salmon is my family's favorite dinner to make at home. To incorporate some more color into the dish, I added purple potatoes, which have a great, nutty flavor that's enhanced by the maple glaze. This is a healthy, protein-packed meal.

SERVES 4

2 tablespoons freshly squeezed lemon juice

2 tablespoons pure maple syrup

1 tablespoon apple cider vinegar

3 tablespoons canola oil, divided

4 (6-ounce) skinless salmon fillets

5 baby purple potatoes (about 8 ounces)

Sea salt and ground white pepper, to taste

3 tablespoons unsalted butter

½ teaspoon salt

¼ teaspoon freshly ground black pepper

4 teaspoons finely grated lemon zest

4 fresh sage sprigs

1. Combine the lemon juice, maple syrup, vinegar, and 1 tablespoon of the oil in a large zip-top bag. Add the salmon, seal the bag, and massage the bag to coat the salmon well with the marinade. Set the bag aside for 10 minutes, turning once.

2. Meanwhile, using a mandoline or very sharp knife, cut the potatoes crosswise into paper-thin slices. In a large skillet, heat the remaining 2 tablespoons of oil over medium heat until it shimmers. Add the potatoes and cook, turning once, for 3 to 4 minutes, until the edges start to brown. Reduce the heat to low to keep them warm while preparing the salmon.

3. Preheat the broiler.

4. Remove the salmon from the bag and pour the marinade into a small saucepan. Heat the marinade over high heat until heated through. Season the salmon with sea salt and white pepper.

5. Heat a large oven-safe nonstick skillet over medium-high heat. Add the salmon fillets and cook for 3 minutes on each side. Brush the hot marinade evenly over the salmon. Transfer the skillet to the broiler and broil for 2 to 3 minutes, until the top of the salmon is caramelized.

6. Meanwhile, add the butter, salt, and black pepper to the potatoes and cook for 2 minutes, or until the butter is melted and the potatoes are heated through.

7. Place 1 salmon fillet on each serving plate. Spoon the potatoes alongside the salmon, garnish with the lemon zest and sage, and serve.

Maple-Glazed Salmon with Baby Purple Potatoes (p. 101)

Potato-Crusted Sausage and Gruyère Quiche

This is one of my favorite hearty breakfasts, and it's quick to prepare. There are many possible variations with this recipe, and you can even swap out the meat entirely for vegetables like bell peppers, mushrooms, tomatoes, and zucchini.

SERVES 4

3 medium russet potatoes, peeled and rinsed

3 tablespoons corn oil

1 teaspoon salt, divided

½ teaspoon freshly ground black pepper, divided

8 ounces bulk pork sausage

1 cup shredded Gruyère

1 (12-ounce) can evaporated milk

2 large eggs

1 tablespoon chopped fresh flat-leaf parsley

Hot pepper sauce (optional)

1. Preheat the oven to 425°F.

2. Using the medium holes of a box grater, shred the potatoes into a bowl. Transfer the shredded potatoes to a clean kitchen towel. Gather the towel and squeeze the potatoes over the sink to remove any excess water. Return the shredded potatoes to the bowl. You should have about 3 cups.

3. Add the oil, ½ teaspoon of the salt, and ¼ teaspoon of the pepper to the potatoes and mix well. Press the mixture evenly into a 9-inch pie pan. Bake the potato crust for 15 to 20 minutes, until beginning to brown.

4. Meanwhile, in a medium skillet, cook the sausage over medium heat, stirring to break up the meat, for about 10 minutes, or until browned. Pour off the drippings.

5. Layer the sausage and cheese in the potato crust. In a small bowl, whisk together the evaporated milk, eggs, remaining ½ teaspoon of salt, and remaining ¼ teaspoon of pepper. Pour the egg mixture over the sausage and cheese. Add the parsley on top. Bake for 30 minutes, or until set and golden brown.

6. Let the quiche cool for 5 minutes. Cut it into wedges and serve with hot sauce, if desired.

Potato-Crusted Shrimp with Tartar Sauce

This dish could technically be eaten as an appetizer or snack, but we usually serve it as a meal with a vegetable side or salad. Instant mashed potatoes probably don't sound super appetizing to you, but they work great in place of panko or breadcrumbs as a crust for the shrimp. Tartar sauce, typically served with fried fish, stands in well here, too. I figured this out when my son, who tried (and liked!) my tartar sauce at the age of five, loved this new pairing.

SERVES 4

4 tablespoons unsalted butter,
    2 tablespoons melted and
    2 tablespoons at room temperature
1 cup instant mashed potato flakes
Salt and freshly ground black pepper
1 pound jumbo shrimp (about 20), peeled
    and deveined

2 lemon wedges
¼ cup chopped fresh flat-leaf parsley, for
    garnish
1 recipe Tartar Sauce (page 177), for dipping

1. Put the melted butter in a shallow dish. Put the potato flakes in a second shallow dish and season with a pinch each of salt and pepper. Dip 1 shrimp into the butter to coat it. Transfer the buttered shrimp to the potato flakes, coating on both sides, and then set it on a plate. Repeat this process with the remaining shrimp.

2. In a large skillet, heat the room-temperature butter over medium heat until the foaming subsides. Working in batches, add the shrimp to the skillet in a single layer and sear on one side for 2 minutes. Flip and sear on the other side for 1 more minute, or until golden brown.

3. Transfer the shrimp to a serving platter. Squeeze the lemon over the shrimp. Garnish with the parsley and serve with the tartar sauce for dipping.

Potato Gnocchi Carbonara with Pancetta (p. 108)

Potato Gnocchi Carbonara with Pancetta

If done right, gnocchi are super light, tender, and perfect for an everyday or special meal. Between all the different sauces and fillings you can use, there are endless ways to make it. This recipe makes twice as much gnocchi as you need, so you can freeze half to use another day for the vegetarian version, Pan-Fried Potato Gnocchi with Spinach (page 135).

SERVES 2–4

½ recipe Potato Gnocchi (page 170), thawed if frozen
2 tablespoons olive oil
3–4 ounces pancetta, chopped
2 cloves garlic, minced
1 shallot, minced
2 tablespoons dry white wine
½ lemon

Salt and freshly ground black pepper, to taste
Red pepper flakes, to taste (optional)
2 large egg yolks
1 small bunch fresh oregano, chopped, for garnish
Grated Parmesan, for garnish

1. Bring a large pot of lightly salted water to a boil over high heat. Add the gnocchi, a few at a time, to the water. When they rise to the surface, use a slotted spoon to transfer them to a colander to drain. Do not overcook them or they will fall apart. When all the gnocchi have cooked and drained, transfer them to a warm serving dish. Reserve ¼ cup of the cooking liquid and set it aside.

2. In a large, deep skillet, heat the olive oil over medium heat. Add the pancetta and sauté for about 5 minutes, or until it crisps up. Using a slotted spoon, transfer the pancetta to paper towels to drain. Reduce the heat to medium-low, add the garlic and shallot to the drippings in the skillet, and sauté for 2 to 3 minutes. Add the wine and cook for another minute, or until the wine has evaporated. Squeeze the juice of the lemon half into the skillet and sauté for 1 minute. Add the gnocchi and pancetta to the skillet and season with salt, black pepper, and red pepper flakes (if using). Remove the skillet from the heat.

3. In a small bowl, whisk together the egg yolks and warm gnocchi cooking liquid to temper the egg yolks. Add the egg mixture to the skillet and mix well.

4. Divide the gnocchi among serving plates. Garnish with the oregano and Parmesan and serve.

The Potatopia Cookbook

Garlicky Potato, Cheddar, and Bacon Pie

This dish is delicious but pretty rich, so I make it once in a while when I have a real craving for it or on special occasions. For my recipe, I added extra garlic and cayenne to kick things up. The dish might seem complicated to make, but after you do it once you'll see how simple it really is. Serve this as a main dish, a hearty side, or as part of a more elaborate brunch.

SERVES 8

2 pounds sliced bacon (not thick-cut)
2 teaspoons light brown sugar, plus more if desired
1 tablespoon freshly ground black pepper, plus more to taste
2 teaspoons cayenne pepper
5 large russet potatoes

Sea salt
1 medium yellow onion, minced
4 cloves garlic, minced
4 cups shredded aged cheddar
1 tablespoon chopped fresh thyme, for garnish

1. Preheat the oven to 350°F. Grease the bottom of a 10- or 12-inch round nonstick baking pan or oven-safe skillet. Cut a circle of parchment paper to fit the bottom of the pan and press it down.

2. Arrange the bacon slices in a bicycle-spoke pattern from the center of the pan so that they sit along the bottom of the pan and continue up and over the sides. Let the ends hang over the edge of the pan. The slices should overlap around the edges of the pan. To make sure the center is not too thick with the bacon, stagger every other piece about 2 inches from the center and extend it farther than the adjacent slices. With the palm of your hand, flatten the center, leaving no gaps in the bacon. Season the bacon with the light brown sugar, black pepper, and cayenne.

3. Using a mandoline or very sharp knife, cut the potatoes crosswise into ¼-inch-thick slices. Arrange the potato slices in a circular pattern of overlapping slices around the inside bottom edge of the pan, on top of the bacon. Continue arranging slightly overlapping circles of the potatoes until the bottom is evenly covered, using about a third of the potatoes for the first layer. Season the potatoes with salt and pepper. Mix the onion and garlic and scatter a third of the mixture over the potatoes. Next add a third of the shredded cheese. Firmly press the layer down and repeat this process twice more for a total of three layers. Set each layer a bit farther away from the edge of the pan than the last. The top should be 1 to 2 inches higher than the pan's rim.

4. Fold the overhanging bacon neatly up and over the top of the potatoes. If desired, sprinkle a bit more light brown sugar and pepper over the bacon. Put a metal lid on top of the pie to weigh it down so the bacon does not shrink too much during the cooking process.

5. Place the pan on a rimmed baking sheet and bake for 2½ to 3 hours, until a small, thin knife inserts easily.

6. Pour off as much of the fat around the edges as possible. Let the pie stand for 15 minutes, then invert it onto a cutting surface. Remove and discard the parchment paper. Slice into wedges, garnish with the thyme, and serve immediately.

Red Wine-Braised Oxtails with Mashed Japanese Yams

I first discovered Japanese yams when I was creating my Marinated Bulgogi recipe (page 97), and I couldn't wait to think of other things to do with them. Once, while browsing the aisles of my favorite Asian market, I noticed oxtails and right away knew they would work in a slow-cooked braise with the yams. Braised oxtails might sound intimidating, but they're no harder to make than traditional braised short ribs—although this recipe has more flavor. It also freezes well if you want to reheat some on a cold night.

SERVES 4

Oxtails

2 pounds beef oxtails, cut into 2-inch pieces
1 teaspoon salt
2 teaspoons freshly ground black pepper
2 tablespoons extra virgin olive oil
2 shallots, chopped
2 large carrots, peeled and cut into 2-inch pieces
4 large celery ribs, cut into 2-inch pieces
1 tablespoon tomato paste
2 large cloves garlic, finely chopped
3½ cups dry red wine
1 cup chicken broth or stock
2 fresh flat-leaf parsley sprigs
1 large fresh rosemary sprig
1 bay leaf

Yams

2 large Japanese yams, peeled, rinsed, and quartered
3 tablespoons unsalted butter
¼ cup light cream or half-and-half
1½ teaspoons salt

Assembly

¼ cup chopped fresh flat-leaf parsley
Finely grated zest of 1 lemon
1 clove garlic, finely chopped
Pinch salt, plus more to taste
Freshly ground black pepper, to taste

1. **For the oxtails:** Rub the oxtails with the salt and pepper and cover with plastic wrap. Refrigerate for at least 2 hours or overnight.

2. Preheat the oven to 325°F.

3. In an 8-quart Dutch oven or a large, heavy saucepan with a lid, heat the oil over medium-high heat until it shimmers. Add as many oxtail pieces as you can fit in a single layer without crowding. Sear, turning occasionally, until the meat is golden brown on all sides, about 1 minute per side. As the oxtails are browned, transfer them to a plate and repeat with the remaining oxtails.

4. Add the shallots to the drippings in the pan, reduce the heat to medium, and cook until the shallots are lightly caramelized, about 5 minutes. Add the carrots and celery and cook for 5 minutes. Stir in the tomato paste and garlic and cook for 1 minute. Add the wine and broth to the pan. Bundle the parsley, rosemary, and bay leaf with kitchen twine and add them to the pan. Bring the mixture to a simmer and cook until the liquid has reduced by half, about 15 minutes.

Recipe continues on next page

5. Return the oxtails to the pan and bring to a simmer. Cover and transfer to the oven. Cook, turning the oxtails every 30 minutes, until the meat is fork tender, 3 to 3½ hours.

6. **For the yams:** During the last 30 minutes of the oxtail cooking time, put the yams in a large saucepan and add enough cold salted water to cover them by 2 inches. Bring to a boil over high heat. Reduce the heat to medium-low and simmer for about 15 minutes, or until a sharp knife easily pierces the yams. Drain the yams and return them to the pan set over low heat. Add the butter, cream, and salt and mash well.

7. **To assemble:** In a small bowl, toss together the parsley, lemon zest, garlic, and salt.

8. Divide the mashed yams evenly among 4 serving plates, mounding them in the center of each. Using tongs, place the oxtails on top of the yams, being careful not to pull the meat off the bones. Remove and discard the herb bundle. Taste the pan juices and add salt and pepper as necessary. Spoon the sauce over the oxtails, garnish with the parsley mixture, and serve.

Chilean Sea Bass with Potatoes Boulangère

Chilean sea bass is my favorite fish to cook and eat—it's delicate and fluffy, but the key is to flavor it properly and take care not to overcook it. I often serve the fish with pommes boulangère, a French potato casserole, for a special meal paired with our favorite bottle of Sauvignon Blanc. You can use another flaky, white fish if you can't find sea bass or prefer something else.

SERVES 4

Potatoes

2 medium to large russet potatoes, peeled and rinsed
6 tablespoons unsalted butter
2 tablespoons canola oil
2 medium yellow onions, thinly sliced
Salt and freshly ground black pepper, to taste

Sea Bass

1 cup dry white wine
⅓ cup chopped shallot
⅓ cup thinly sliced fresh ginger
½ cup heavy cream
⅓ cup soy sauce
3 tablespoons honey
1 tablespoon rice vinegar
1½ tablespoons cold water
1½ teaspoons cornstarch
4 (6-ounce) sea bass fillets, skinned if desired
4 tablespoons unsalted butter, chilled and cut into small pieces
Salt and freshly ground black pepper, to taste
4 fresh thyme sprigs, for garnish

1. Preheat the oven to 375°F.

2. **For the potatoes:** Using a mandoline or very sharp knife, cut the potatoes crosswise into paper-thin slices. Set aside.

3. In a large skillet, heat the butter with the oil over medium heat until the foaming subsides. Add the onions and sauté until they are golden and soft but not brown, about 5 minutes. Using tongs or a slotted spoon, transfer the onions to a bowl and reserve the melted butter in the skillet.

4. Liberally brush some of the melted butter in the bottom of a shallow 2-quart oval baking dish. Arrange a layer of the potatoes in the dish, followed by a layer of the onions. Season with salt and pepper, then dot about 1 tablespoon of the melted butter over the onions. Repeat this process until you have used all the potatoes and onions, ending with a layer of the potatoes. Season with more salt and pepper and drizzle any of the remaining melted butter over the top. Pour in just enough water to reach the top of the potatoes.

5. Bake for 30 to 40 minutes, until the liquid has been absorbed and the potatoes are tender.

Recipe continues on next page

6. **For the sea bass:** Meanwhile, in a small heavy saucepan, combine the wine, shallot, and ginger over high heat. Bring to a boil and cook until the liquid is reduced to ¼ cup, about 5 minutes. Add the cream and boil until the liquid is reduced by half, about 3 minutes. Remove from the heat. Set the sauce aside.

7. In a separate small, heavy saucepan, combine the soy sauce, honey, and rice vinegar. In a small bowl, whisk together the water and cornstarch until smooth. Add the cornstarch mixture to the soy sauce mixture. Stir the mixture over medium heat until the glaze boils and thickens slightly, 2 to 3 minutes. Remove from the heat and set aside to cool to room temperature.

8. Arrange the fillets on a rimmed baking sheet. Brush with some of the glaze. About 15 minutes before the potatoes are done, place the fish in the oven with the potatoes. Bake for 12 to 15 minutes, until the fish is opaque. Remove from the oven. Bring the remaining glaze to a boil over low heat. Spoon the glaze over the fish. By this point, the potatoes should be done. Remove them from the oven and set aside.

9. Bring the sauce to a simmer over low heat. Remove from the heat and gradually add the chilled butter, a few pieces at a time, whisking just until melted before adding more. Strain the sauce through a fine-mesh sieve. Season with salt and pepper.

10. Spoon the sauce equally onto each of 4 serving plates. Top with the fish and a slice of the potatoes boulangère. Garnish with the thyme sprigs and serve immediately.

Waxy Potatoes with Crème Fraîche and Lemon-Caper Veal Scaloppine

Baby Red Bliss potatoes have a low starch content and a creamy, firm texture that helps the potatoes hold their shape after cooking, making for a beautiful presentation.

SERVES 4

18–24 baby Red Bliss potatoes (about 2½ pounds)
⅓ cup crème fraîche
½ teaspoon salt, divided, plus more to taste
½ teaspoon freshly ground black pepper, divided, plus more to taste
1 pound veal cutlets, ⅛–¼ inch thick
⅓ cup all-purpose flour
6 teaspoons extra virgin olive oil, divided, plus more for garnish

2 large leeks, white and light green parts only, thinly sliced
1 cup chicken broth or stock
3 cloves garlic, minced
2 tablespoons capers, rinsed
1 teaspoon finely grated lemon zest
1 tablespoon freshly squeezed lemon juice
3 tablespoons chopped fresh flat-leaf parsley
Grated Parmesan or Pecorino Romano, for garnish (optional)

1. Put the potatoes in a large saucepan and add enough cold salted water to cover them by 2 inches. Bring to a boil over high heat. Reduce the heat to medium and simmer for about 15 minutes, or until a sharp knife easily pierces the potatoes. Drain the potatoes in a colander. When the potatoes are cool enough to handle, carefully remove and discard the skins. Using a mandoline or very sharp knife, cut the potatoes crosswise into ¼-inch-thick slices.

2. In a large skillet, heat the crème fraîche over medium heat until hot but not boiling. Add the potatoes and season with salt and pepper. Remove the skillet from the heat and cover with aluminum foil to keep the potatoes warm until serving time.

3. While the potatoes are boiling, season the cutlets on both sides with ¼ teaspoon each of the salt and pepper. Put the flour on a large plate. Dredge the cutlets in the flour, shaking off the excess.

4. In a large nonstick skillet, heat 2 teaspoons of the oil over medium heat until it shimmers. Add half of the cutlets and cook until golden brown and just cooked through, 1 to 3 minutes per side. Transfer the cutlets to a platter and tent with foil. Add 2 more teaspoons of the oil to the pan and cook the remaining cutlets. Transfer to the platter.

5. Add the remaining 2 teaspoons of oil to the pan. Add the leeks and cook, stirring occasionally, until they are soft and light brown, 6 to 8 minutes. Stir in the broth and garlic. Bring to a boil, scraping up any brown bits, and simmer for 2 minutes. Stir in the capers, lemon zest, lemon juice, parsley, and remaining ¼ teaspoon each of salt and pepper.

6. Return the cutlets and any accumulated juices to the pan. Cook, turning the veal to coat with the sauce, until heated through, 1 to 2 minutes.

7. Divide the cutlets among 4 serving plates and top each with some of the leek mixture. Garnish with a few drops of olive oil and a bit of Parmesan, if desired. Spoon the potatoes alongside the veal and serve.

Rib-Eye Steaks with Potato Cream Sauce (p. 118)

Rib-Eye Steaks with Potato Cream Sauce

This dish started with the potato cream sauce—it makes a fabulous complement to steak in place of the herbed butter topping and traditional mashed or baked potato side you might find at a typical steak house. Now it's hard to go back. The cream sauce can be made two days prior and refrigerated, then reheated just before serving.

SERVES 6

Potato Cream Sauce

4 tablespoons olive oil, divided
3 medium shallots, thinly sliced
1 fresh thyme sprig
2 medium Yukon Gold potatoes, cut into
    ½-inch cubes (about 1½ cups)
1 teaspoon kosher salt, plus more to taste
Pinch red pepper flakes
1 cup chicken broth or stock
2 tablespoons whole milk, plus more as
    needed
⅓ cup crème fraîche
⅓ cup mayonnaise

Steaks and Asparagus

3 (12- to 14-ounce) boneless rib-eye steaks,
    halved crosswise
Sea salt and freshly ground black pepper,
    to taste
18–20 asparagus spears
3 tablespoons extra virgin olive oil, divided
⅓ cup water
2 tablespoons unsalted butter
Small bunch watercress, for garnish

1. Preheat the oven to 350°F.

2. **For the potato cream sauce:** In a medium oven-safe skillet, heat 2 tablespoons of the oil over medium heat until it shimmers. Add the shallots and thyme and cook, stirring occasionally, until the shallots are wilted but not brown, about 5 minutes. Add the potatoes, salt, and red pepper flakes and cook, stirring occasionally, for about 5 minutes. The potatoes will still be slightly undercooked. Transfer the skillet to the oven and roast the potatoes until tender, about 20 minutes.

3. Transfer the potatoes to a blender. Add the broth and milk and purée. With the blender running on low speed, slowly add the remaining 2 tablespoons of oil, increasing the speed as you go, and blend until the sauce is emulsified.

4. Pass the sauce through a fine-mesh strainer into a medium bowl. Whisk in the crème fraîche and mayonnaise. Taste and add salt as needed. Set aside until ready to serve.

5. **For the steaks and asparagus:** Season the steaks with salt and pepper.

6. Remove and discard the tough ends of the asparagus spears. Using a vegetable peeler, peel the skin from the bottom half of each spear. In a large skillet, heat 1 tablespoon of the oil over medium heat until it shimmers. Add the asparagus and water. Season with sea salt. Cover, cook for 10 minutes, and set aside.

7. Meanwhile, in another large skillet, heat the remaining 2 tablespoons of oil and the butter over high heat until the foaming subsides. Add the steaks and sear on both sides, 1 to 2 minutes per side. Transfer the skillet to the oven and bake for 6 to 8 minutes, until an instant-read thermometer inserted into the thickest part of the steak registers 135° to 140°F for medium.

8. Just before serving, reheat the potato cream sauce in a saucepan over medium-low heat, stirring frequently, until heated through and smooth. (You can add 1 tablespoon of milk to loosen it up, if needed.) Place 1 steak on each serving plate. Generously spoon the warmed potato cream sauce over the steaks. Place the cooked asparagus next to the steak and garnish with sprigs of watercress.

Chicken Potato Pot Pie

One chilly night, my family and I were looking for something hearty to warm us up. Pot pie came to mind, and I decided to add my favorite food to the dish. I chose red-skinned potatoes to add a little earthy flavor and richness.

SERVES 4–6

8 tablespoons (1 stick) unsalted butter
½ cup all-purpose flour
4 cups chicken broth or stock
Salt and freshly ground black pepper, to taste
Pinch cayenne pepper
3 tablespoons heavy cream, divided
2 pounds cooked boneless, skinless chicken breast or thighs, shredded
6–8 medium red potatoes, cut into ½-inch pieces (about 8 ounces)

2 large celery roots, peeled and cut into ½-inch pieces (about 8 ounces)
1–2 medium parsnips, peeled and cut into ½-inch pieces (about 8 ounces)
1 medium yellow onion, diced
2 cloves garlic, minced
1 sheet frozen puff pastry, thawed per package instructions
1 large egg

1. In a large saucepan, melt the butter over medium heat until the foaming subsides. Add the flour and whisk to ensure there are no lumps. Add the chicken broth. Cook the mixture, stirring occasionally, for 5 minutes. Check the consistency of the sauce by dipping the back of a spoon into it and running your finger along the spoon. You want the sauce to cling to the spoon and not run over the swipe you made. Season with salt, black pepper, and cayenne.

2. Add 2 tablespoons of the cream and stir to combine. Stir in the chicken, potatoes, celery roots, parsnips, onion, and garlic and cook for 2 to 3 minutes. Transfer the filling to a bowl and refrigerate for 1 hour, or until cool.

3. Preheat the oven to 400°F.

4. Roll out the puff pastry on a lightly floured work surface so that a 9- to 11-inch bowl or plate just fits on the dough. Cut the dough around the bowl; this ensures that your dough is large enough to fit over your baking dish. Spoon the chilled filling into a shallow 8- to 10-inch round baking dish.

5. In a small bowl, whisk the egg and remaining 1 tablespoon of cream. Brush some of the egg wash on the edges of the baking dish. Lay the puff pastry over the top, being careful not to stretch the pastry. Seal the edges of the pastry by lightly pushing them onto the rim of the dish to make sure they are secure. Brush the top evenly with more of the egg wash.

6. Place the dish on a rimmed baking sheet and bake for 25 to 35 minutes, until the pastry is a deep golden brown. Remove from the oven and let cool for 5 minutes before serving.

The Potatopia Cookbook

Mashed Potato Meatballs over Arugula Salad

Meatballs can be found in various forms in all cuisines. In Italy meatballs are often eaten with spaghetti and red sauce, in Russia they're eaten with barley, and in China many people enjoy them with dumplings. I wanted to incorporate potatoes into meatballs without making them heavy. Here the meatball taste shines with just that hint of earthy, creamy potatoes, further lightened by a bright, crisp arugula salad.

SERVES 4

2 medium russet potatoes, peeled, rinsed, and cut into chunks

8 ounces lean ground beef

8 ounces lean ground veal

2 slices mortadella, diced

1 large egg

6 tablespoons grated Parmesan, divided

4 tablespoons chopped fresh flat-leaf parsley, divided

Salt and freshly ground pepper, to taste

1 cup plain or seasoned dry breadcrumbs

7 tablespoons extra virgin olive oil, divided

5 ounces arugula

1 tablespoon freshly squeezed lemon juice

1. Put the potatoes in a large saucepan and add enough cold salted water to cover them by 2 inches. Bring to a boil over high heat. Reduce the heat to medium and simmer for about 15 minutes, or until a sharp knife easily pierces the potatoes. Drain the potatoes and transfer them to a large bowl. Using a potato masher, mash them while they are still hot.

2. Add the beef, veal, mortadella, and egg, stirring to mix well. Stir in 2 tablespoons of the Parmesan and 2 tablespoons of the parsley. Season with salt and pepper. Using your hands, form the mixture into meatballs the size of golf balls. Put the breadcrumbs in a shallow dish. Roll each meatball in the breadcrumbs to coat.

3. In a large skillet, heat 3 tablespoons of the olive oil over medium heat until it shimmers. Add the meatballs and cook, turning frequently, until golden brown all over and cooked through, about 2 minutes per side. Using a slotted spoon, transfer the meatballs to paper towels to drain.

4. In a large bowl, toss the arugula with the remaining 4 tablespoons of olive oil and the lemon juice. Season with salt and pepper. Add 2 tablespoons of the Parmesan and toss well. Divide the salad evenly among 4 serving plates. Arrange the meatballs on top and garnish with the remaining 2 tablespoons of Parmesan and 2 tablespoons of parsley. Serve right away.

Sake Short Rib Potato Stew

I based this recipe on shikoya, a hearty, delicious Russian potato and meat stew dish that made a frequent appearance on my dinner table growing up. As Asian is one of my favorite cuisines, I decided to give shikoya that flavorful spin using sake, umami-rich bonito flakes, soy sauce, and sesame, plus Asian vegetables like bok choy.

SERVES 4

2 pounds boneless beef short ribs

Sea salt and freshly ground black pepper, to taste

1/3 cup extra virgin olive oil

5 cloves garlic, minced

1 medium shallot, minced

2 cups beef broth or stock

1/2 cup sake

1 teaspoon bonito flakes

3 tablespoons soy sauce

2 tablespoons chili oil

2 tablespoons toasted sesame oil

1 tablespoon rice vinegar

2 teaspoons granulated sugar

1 1/2 teaspoons Chinese five-spice powder

3 medium russet potatoes, peeled and rinsed

3 tablespoons canola oil

1 cup diced celery

3–4 baby bok choy

1 1/2 cups sliced scallions, divided

1/2 cup canned drained sliced water chestnuts

3 (2-inch) chunks fresh ginger, peeled

1/2 cup chopped fresh cilantro

1 bunch bean sprouts

1. Preheat the oven to 375°F.

2. Season the short ribs with salt and pepper. In a 6-quart Dutch oven or oven-safe stockpot, heat the olive oil over medium-high heat until it shimmers. Add the short ribs and brown on all sides, about 5 minutes. Using tongs, transfer the ribs to a plate.

3. Reduce the heat to medium, add the garlic and shallot, and sauté for 2 minutes. Add the beef broth and bring to a simmer. Stir in the sake and bonito flakes and continue to simmer for 2 minutes. Add the soy sauce, chili oil, sesame oil, rice vinegar, sugar, and five-spice powder. Cook, stirring occasionally, for 6 to 8 minutes.

4. Return the short ribs and any accumulated juices to the pot. Cover and bake for 1 1/2 hours.

5. While the short ribs cook, cut the potatoes lengthwise into 1/2-inch-thick slices. Stack the slices and cut lengthwise again into 1-inch-thick steak fries. In a 14-inch skillet, heat the canola oil over medium heat until it shimmers. Add the potatoes, season with salt, and cook until they are browned on all sides but not cooked through. Set aside.

6. After the ribs have baked for 1 1/2 hours, turn them and continue baking, covered, for 15 minutes. Add the potatoes to the pot, stir gently, and continue baking, covered, for about 45 minutes, or until the short ribs and potatoes are tender but not falling apart.

Recipe continues on next page

7. Transfer the Dutch oven to the stovetop over low heat. Add the celery, bok choy, 1 cup of the scallions, and the water chestnuts. Put the ginger in a garlic press or handheld juicer and squeeze the ginger juices into the stew. Very gently stir the stew, taking care not to break the potatoes. Cook for only 4 more minutes; this will keep the crunch in the water chestnuts and celery.

8. Using a large spoon, transfer the short ribs to serving plates or shallow bowls (the meat will be very tender). Spoon the sauce with the potatoes and vegetables over the meat. Garnish the stew with the cilantro, the remaining ½ cup of scallions, and the bean sprouts. Serve right away.

Whole-Roasted Branzino with Smoked Potatoes

This is one my favorite dishes of all time, especially when I am on a diet, as it's super healthy and easy to prepare. I'm always one to add butter to my potatoes, but you can cut back on the butter if you want, as smoking the potatoes imparts double the flavor and brings the humble vegetable to a whole new level.

SERVES 4–6

Potatoes
4 medium russet potatoes, well scrubbed
2–3 tablespoons unsalted butter, melted
Coarse sea salt and freshly ground black pepper, to taste

Branzino
2 (14- to 16-ounce) whole branzinos, cleaned and gutted
Extra virgin olive oil, for brushing

Sea salt and freshly ground black pepper, to taste
6 fresh flat-leaf parsley sprigs
6 fresh thyme sprigs
1 lemon, thinly sliced
2 cloves garlic, thinly sliced
Butter, sour cream, chopped fresh chives, or anything you love on a potato, for serving

1. **For the potatoes:** Soak 2 to 3 cups of hickory woodchips in cold water for 1 hour, then drain them. Set up a grill for indirect grilling and preheat it to high. If using a gas grill, place all the wood chips in the smoker box or in a smoker pouch and preheat until you see smoke. (If using a charcoal grill, wait until you are ready to cook and then toss the chips onto the hot coals.)

2. Using a fork, prick each potato several times. Brush the potatoes all over with the melted butter. Season very generously with salt and pepper.

3. Place the potatoes on the grill in the center of the hot grate, away from the heat, and cover the grill. Smoke-roast the potatoes, turning once, for 1 to 1¼ hours, until a sharp knife easily pierces the potatoes and the skins are crisp. (If using a charcoal grill and the potatoes are not done after 1 hour, add 12 fresh coals and ½ cup of soaked wood chips to each side of the grill.)

4. **For the branzino:** After the potatoes have cooked for 1 hour, use a sharp knife to cut several diagonal slits on both sides of each fish. Brush the fish inside and out with olive oil. Season the fish inside and out with salt and pepper. Stuff the cavities with the parsley, thyme, lemon slices, and garlic. You may want to use twine to close the fish to keep the lemon and herbs in place while turning.

5. Move the potatoes to the outer edges of the grill and brush the grate generously with oil. Place the fish on the grill over direct heat. Cover and cook for about 6 minutes on each side, or until grill marks appear. Do not try to flip the fish sooner as the skin might tear.

6. Transfer the fish to serving plates. Add the smoked potatoes. Serve the potatoes with your favorite toppings.

Sesame-Marinated Chicken with Golden Dutch Potatoes

There's something strangely addicting about Cantonese-style sesame chicken. Instead of pairing it with rice, I wondered how I could use potatoes in the dish. Did you know that in the northern parts of China, potatoes—particularly gold potatoes—are used in a variety of dishes, even more than rice? In some cases, potatoes are paired with truffles, similar to how the French enjoy them. In this case, I paired the nutty sesame chicken with another European style of preparing golden potatoes.

SERVES 4

Marinade
¼ cup olive oil
2 tablespoons cream cheese
1 teaspoon rice vinegar
1 teaspoon soy sauce
½ teaspoon freshly squeezed lemon juice
1 teaspoon freshly ground black pepper
½ teaspoon salt
½ teaspoon cayenne pepper
2 (3 x 3-inch) roasted sesame-flavored nori sheets
3 cloves garlic, coarsely chopped

Chicken
1 (3½-pound) whole chicken
Sesame seeds

Potatoes
18–20 baby Yukon Gold or baby Yellow Dutch potatoes (5–6 pounds)
1 cup water
2 fresh thyme sprigs
2 fresh oregano sprigs
1 bay leaf
2 teaspoons salt
1 teaspoon paprika
6 tablespoons unsalted butter, melted
3 tablespoons crème fraîche
1 tablespoon minced garlic

Assembly
Chopped fresh basil or Thai basil, for garnish
Sea salt, to taste

1. **For the marinade:** In a food processor, combine all the ingredients and process until blended. Set aside.

2. **For the chicken:** Put the chicken in a large zip-top bag. Pour the marinade evenly over the chicken, seal the bag, and refrigerate for 1 to 3 hours.

3. Preheat the oven to 400°F.

4. Remove the chicken from the marinade and place it on a wire rack set in a shallow roasting pan; this will ensure even cooking on the bottom. Bake for 30 minutes. Remove from the oven and evenly sprinkle sesame seeds all over the chicken. Continue baking until an instant-read thermometer inserted into the thickest part of the thigh (but not touching the bone) registers 165°F and the chicken skin is crisp. Transfer to a cutting board and let the chicken rest for 5 minutes before carving.

5. **For the potatoes:** While the chicken finishes cooking, combine the potatoes, water, thyme, oregano, bay leaf, salt, and paprika in a large cast iron skillet. Bring to a boil over medium-high heat. Reduce the heat to medium, cover, and cook until a sharp knife easily pierces the potatoes, 10 to 15 minutes. Drain the potatoes and remove and discard the thyme, oregano, and bay leaf. Add the butter, crème fraîche, and garlic and stir well until the potatoes are coated.

6. **To assemble:** Transfer the chicken to a serving platter. Arrange the potatoes around the edges. Sprinkle basil and sea salt over the potatoes. Serve right away.

Herb and Brown Butter Scallops with Thick-Cut Potato Chips

Scallops are a favorite of Alex's, one of my business partners. He always orders them when we eat out. Here, I partner—pun intended—tender scallops with my sturdy, thick-cut potato chips, the base for a one-bite explosion.

SERVES 4

1 tablespoon olive oil

1 pound fresh sea scallops, side muscles removed

Kosher salt and freshly ground black pepper, to taste

2 tablespoons unsalted butter, cut into small pieces

1 fresh thyme sprig, stem removed and leaves coarsely chopped

1 fresh sage sprig, stem removed and leaves coarsely chopped

1 fresh rosemary sprig, stem removed and leaves coarsely chopped

1 fresh tarragon sprig, stem removed and leaves coarsely chopped

2 teaspoons freshly squeezed lemon juice

1 recipe Homemade Thick-Cut Potato Chips (page 172)

1. Heat the oil in a large skillet over medium-high heat until it shimmers. Season the scallops with salt and pepper and cook until they are a deep golden brown on 1 side, about 3 minutes. Turn the scallops and add the butter and two-thirds of the herbs to the skillet. Continue cooking, spooning the butter over the scallops often, until the scallops are cooked through and the butter is brown and smells nutty, about 3 minutes. Add the lemon juice.

2. Place 1 scallop on top of each potato slice. Drizzle the browned butter sauce over all and garnish with the extra chips and remaining fresh herbs.

CHAPTER 4:
Meatless Mains

Whether it's for environmental reasons, health concerns, or personal preferences, many of us are consciously trying to eat less meat. Despite the common "meat and potatoes" refrain, with potatoes, there's not always a need for meat. Not only do they come packed with as much protein as some beans, they're just as filling as meat in their own right.

Layered Mashed Potato and Truffled Mushroom Casserole

This robust casserole is an homage to my father, who is a chef by trade and makes one of the best mushroom sauces I've ever tasted. When we gather for family meals, more often than not he serves mashed potatoes. We make a well in the center, spoon the mushroom sauce into it, and dig in. This casserole, which easily feeds a big family, uses all the same flavors. By the way, this mushroom sauce is my own; my father has never shared his recipe!

SERVES 10-12

Potatoes
6 medium russet potatoes, peeled, rinsed, and quartered
½ cup light cream or half-and-half
1 teaspoon salt

Breadcrumbs
¼ (18- to 20-inch) fresh baguette, torn into several pieces
¼ cup shredded Pecorino Romano

Mushroom Sauce
1 tablespoon corn oil
1 cup chopped yellow onion
2 tablespoons minced garlic
1¼ pounds baby portabella (cremini) mushrooms, trimmed and minced (about 6 cups)
¼ cup dry red wine
¼ cup light cream or half-and-half
6 ounces Gruyère, shredded
Salt and freshly ground black pepper, to taste

Assembly
Black truffle oil, for garnish
Chopped scallions or fresh chives, for garnish
3 slices bacon, cooked crisp and crumbled, for garnish (optional)

1. **For the potatoes:** Put the potatoes in a large saucepan and add enough cold salted water to cover them by 2 inches. Bring to a boil over high heat. Reduce the heat to medium and simmer for about 15 minutes, or until a sharp knife easily pierces the potatoes. Drain the potatoes and return them to the saucepan, off the heat. Using a potato masher, mash the potatoes while they are still hot. (Alternatively, you can put them through a ricer.)

2. In a small saucepan, heat the cream over medium heat. Stir until it starts to steam and small bubbles form around the edge of the pan. Pour the hot cream over the potatoes and stir to mix. Add the salt and stir until well blended. Set the potatoes aside to cool to room temperature.

3. **For the breadcrumbs:** While the potatoes cool, put the baguette pieces in the bowl of a food processor and pulse a few times to make coarse crumbs. Add the Pecorino Romano and pulse to make fine breadcrumbs.

4. Preheat the oven to 400°F.

Recipe continues on next page

5. **For the mushroom sauce:** In a large skillet, heat the oil over medium-high heat until it shimmers. Add the onion and sauté for 2 minutes. Add the garlic and continue cooking for 2 to 3 minutes, until the onion softens. Add the mushrooms and sauté for 5 more minutes, or until the mushrooms soften and release their liquid.

6. Add the wine and cook, stirring occasionally, for 3 to 4 minutes, until the mixture has slightly reduced. Add the cream and cook, stirring occasionally, for 3 minutes, or until the cream starts to form small bubbles. Stir in the Gruyère and cook until the cheese and mushrooms are well mixed and the cheese melts. Season with salt and pepper.

7. **To assemble:** Evenly spread half of the potatoes in a 12-inch oval baking dish. Top the potatoes with half of the mushroom sauce. Repeat this process with the remaining potatoes and mushroom sauce. Top with the breadcrumb mixture. Bake for 8 to 10 minutes, until heated through.

8. Remove the casserole from the oven and preheat the broiler. Broil the casserole 3 to 4 inches from the heat for 4 to 5 minutes, until nicely browned.

9. Drizzle the casserole with truffle oil and garnish with chopped scallions. Top with the crumbled bacon, if desired, and serve immediately.

Pan-Fried Potato Gnocchi with Spinach

This recipe is a vegetarian-friendly spin-off of my Potato Gnocchi Carbonara with Pancetta (page 108). Here the gnocchi are pan-fried for extra flavor and texture. If the uncooked gnocchi dough was previously frozen, be sure to thaw it completely before boiling; otherwise the outsides can cook faster than the insides.

SERVES 2–4

½ recipe Potato Gnocchi (page 170), thawed if frozen
8 tablespoons olive oil, divided
1 pound fresh spinach leaves
Salt and freshly ground black pepper, to taste

3 tablespoons unsalted butter, cut into pieces
Grated Pecorino Romano, for garnish

1. Bring a large pot of lightly salted water to a boil over high heat. Add the gnocchi, a few at a time, to the water. When they rise to the surface, use a slotted spoon to transfer them to a colander to drain. Do not overcook them or they will fall apart. When all the gnocchi have cooked and drained, transfer them to a warm serving dish. Reserve ¼ cup of the cooking liquid and set it aside.

2. In a large skillet, heat 3 tablespoons of the olive oil over medium heat until it shimmers. Add the spinach and cook, turning with tongs, until it is wilted and reduced by half. Season with salt and pepper. Transfer the spinach to a plate.

3. Add the remaining 5 tablespoons of olive oil to the skillet and heat over medium heat until it shimmers. Add the gnocchi and pan-fry them for about 2 minutes on each side, or until golden brown and crisp. Return the spinach to the skillet. Add the butter and cook, stirring until the butter melts. Season with salt and pepper.

4. Transfer the gnocchi to serving plates, garnish with cheese, and serve.

Potato, Mascarpone, and Mushroom Stuffed Crêpes

You could make a whole meal out of these crêpes or serve them as a side dish with grilled steak or salmon. As a fan of traditional crêpes, I used a flavorful sauce of wine, cream, mushrooms, and plenty of garlic to complement the potato filling. The rest was history.

SERVES 4

½ cup extra virgin olive oil
4 cloves garlic, chopped
1 shallot, chopped
8 ounces baby portabella (cremini) mushrooms, stemmed and chopped
¼ cup dry white wine
1 cup light cream or half-and-half
3 tablespoons Tuscan seasoning or Italian seasoning

2 tablespoons mascarpone cheese
¼ teaspoon salt
¼ teaspoon freshly ground black pepper
4 Basic Crêpes (recipe follows) or store-bought crêpes
2 cups Creamy Mashed Potatoes (page 166), chilled or at room temperature
¼ cup grated Parmesan

1. Preheat the oven to 400°F. Grease a 13 × 9-inch baking dish.

2. In a 12- to 14-inch skillet, heat the olive oil over medium-high heat until it shimmers. Add the garlic and shallot and cook, stirring occasionally, for 5 minutes, or until the shallot softens. Take care that the garlic does not burn. Add the mushrooms and cook, stirring occasionally, for 5 to 7 minutes, until the mushrooms soften and release their liquid.

3. Add the wine and cook, stirring occasionally, for 4 to 5 minutes, until the liquid evaporates. Stir in the cream and Tuscan seasoning and cook for about 2 more minutes, or until the cream is hot but not yet bubbling. Add the mascarpone and stir until the sauce is smooth and creamy. Season with the salt and pepper. Remove from the heat, cover, and set aside, stirring several times to prevent overthickening.

4. Place 1 crêpe on a work surface. Spread about ½ cup of the mashed potatoes on one side of the crêpe. Spoon 2 to 3 tablespoons of the mushroom sauce over the potatoes. Roll the crêpe into a cylinder. Transfer the rolled crêpe, seam side down, to the prepared baking dish. Repeat this process to roll 3 more crêpes, arranging the stuffed crêpes in a snug single layer.

5. Spoon the remaining mushroom sauce over the top of the crêpes. Sprinkle with the Parmesan and bake for about 10 minutes, or until the cheese melts and starts to brown. Serve immediately.

Basic Crêpes

MAKES ABOUT 20 CRÊPES

1½ cups sifted all-purpose flour
1 cup whole milk
1 cup water
2 large eggs

1 teaspoon salt
1 teaspoon granulated sugar
2 tablespoons unsalted butter, plus more as needed

1. In a blender, combine the flour, milk, water, eggs, salt, and sugar. Process until the mixture is smooth and bubbles form, about 30 seconds. Let the batter sit for at least 15 minutes or refrigerate for up to 1 day and whisk before using.

2. In a 12-inch nonstick skillet, heat the butter over medium heat until the foaming subsides. Add ⅓ cup of the batter and swirl the skillet to completely cover the bottom with the batter. Cook until the underside of the crêpe is golden brown, 2 to 3 minutes.

3. Using a rubber spatula, loosen the edge of the crêpe. Then, with your fingertips, quickly flip it and cook for 1 more minute. Slide the crêpe out of the skillet onto a paper towel–lined plate. Repeat this process with the remaining batter, adding more butter to the pan as needed to prevent sticking.

4. To store the crêpes, wrap the stack tightly in plastic wrap and store in a large zip-top bag in the refrigerator for up to 4 days or in the freezer for up to 3 months. To reheat, allow them to thaw and then, one at a time, microwave each crêpe for 15 to 30 seconds.

Cheesy Red Potato Casserole with Croutons and Chives

Low on groceries one day during the dead of winter, we had little in our cabinets, but I was determined to make a satisfying meal—this recipe is the result. Turning the pantry into a culinary "mystery box" is one way to add some excitement to your day, for sure. Turns out, my kids absolutely fell in love with this dish. Two points for saving some extra cash.

SERVES 6-8

25–30 baby red potatoes (about 3 pounds)
2 cups croutons (I prefer cheese-seasoned white croutons.)
3 cups shredded cheddar
¼ cup mayonnaise
2 teaspoons olive oil

4 tablespoons unsalted butter
¼ cup light cream or half-and-half
¼ cup sour cream
Salt and freshly ground black pepper, to taste
1 bunch fresh chives, thinly sliced

1. Preheat the oven to 400°F.

2. Put the potatoes in a large saucepan and add enough cold salted water to cover them by 2 inches. Bring to a boil over high heat. Reduce the heat to medium and simmer for about 30 minutes, or until a sharp knife easily pierces the potatoes.

3. While the potatoes cook, put the croutons in a food processor and pulse until they are coarsely chopped. Transfer the croutons to a bowl and add the cheese, mayonnaise, and olive oil and mix well. Set aside.

4. When the potatoes are tender, drain them in a colander. Return them to the pan and add the butter, cream, and sour cream. Using a potato masher, mash the potatoes well while they are still hot. Season with salt and pepper.

5. Spread the mashed potatoes evenly in a shallow 1½-quart casserole dish. Sprinkle the crouton mixture evenly over the potatoes. Transfer the dish to the oven and bake for 10 minutes, or until the potatoes are heated through and the topping is golden brown. If the topping does not brown, turn on the broiler and broil just until browned.

6. Let the casserole stand for about 3 minutes. Cut it into squares, garnish with the chives, and serve.

Potato Puffs with Zesty Sour Cream

This take on Tater Tots features olives, relish, and corn for a flavorful departure from the norm. The quick and easy sauce adds a tangy kick and can be used for other potato dishes, too.

SERVES 6–8

2 ears corn, shucked

2 tablespoons extra virgin olive oil

1 teaspoon chili powder

1 teaspoon sea salt, divided, plus more to taste

1 teaspoon freshly ground black pepper, divided

3 medium russet potatoes, peeled and rinsed

1 large egg

1 small shallot, chopped

Rice bran or other neutral vegetable oil, for frying

½ cup chopped Vidalia or other sweet onion

½ cup chopped pitted olives

¼ cup hot pepper relish

2 cups shredded extra sharp cheddar

2 cups shredded smoked Gouda

1 recipe Zesty Sour Cream (page 177), for serving

Chopped fresh chives, for garnish

Chopped fresh cilantro, for garnish

1 ripe avocado, halved, pitted, and cubed, for garnish

1 jalapeño, seeded and minced, for garnish (optional)

1. Preheat the oven to 375°F.

2. Cut the corn kernels from the cobs and put them in a medium bowl. Add the olive oil, chili powder, and ½ teaspoon each of the salt and pepper and mix well. Spread the corn mixture onto a rimmed baking sheet. Bake for 10 to 15 minutes, until slightly browned.

3. Meanwhile, using the small holes of a box grater, grate the potatoes directly into a bowl of cold water. Drain and transfer the grated potatoes to a clean kitchen towel. Gather the towel and squeeze the potatoes over the sink to remove any excess water. Return them to the dry bowl. Stir in the egg, shallot, and remaining ½ teaspoon each of salt and pepper and mix well. Shape a small handful of the mixture into a 2 × 1-inch cylinder. Repeat this process with the remaining mixture.

4. In a large saucepan, heat 2 inches of rice bran oil over medium heat until it shimmers and a deep-fry thermometer registers 375°F. Working in batches so as not to crowd the pan, add a handful of the potato puffs and fry for about 2 minutes, or until golden brown. Stir the potato puffs with tongs to prevent them from sticking together. Using a slotted spoon, transfer the potato puffs to paper towels to drain, and season with salt while hot. Allow the oil to regain temperature between batches.

5. Transfer the potato puffs to a pie plate or shallow oven-safe casserole dish. Top with the corn mixture, onion, olives and hot pepper relish. Sprinkle the cheddar and Gouda over all.

6. Preheat the broiler. Place the plate 6 to 8 inches from the heat source and broil for 3 to 5 minutes, watching closely so the cheese does not burn.

7. Remove from the oven and drizzle the sour cream over all. Garnish with the chives, cilantro, avocado, and jalapeño, if desired. Serve right away.

CHAPTER 5:
Sides

When we think of potato-based sides, most of us picture the usual suspects: mashed potatoes, cheesy potato casseroles, and more. While I have included those recipes, you'll also find some more imaginative creations meant to be eaten in a supporting role—but those rules can always be broken.

Aligot

Here's the base for my delicious Aligot Croquettes (page 32). This dish is a perfect accompaniment to any protein or even vegetable. Typically eaten in and around the Pyrenees Mountains of the South of France, aligot incorporates the use of a potato ricer and fondue-like cheese blend of mozzarella and Gruyère for a slightly elastic consistency and rich flavor.

SERVES 2

4 large Yukon Gold potatoes, peeled, rinsed, and diced
½ cup heavy cream
¼ cup whole milk
1 clove garlic, minced

1 cup shredded mozzarella
1 cup shredded Gruyère
Kosher salt and freshly ground black pepper, to taste

1. Put the potatoes in a large saucepan and add enough cold salted water to cover them by 2 inches. Bring to a boil over high heat. Reduce the heat to medium and simmer for about 20 minutes, or until a sharp knife easily pierces the potatoes. Drain the potatoes in a colander.

2. Combine the cream, milk, and garlic in the same saucepan set over low heat. Force the potatoes through a potato ricer into the mixture and stir with a wooden spoon to combine. If you don't have a potato ricer, use a fork to mash the potatoes with the cream, milk, and garlic mixture until creamy. Add the cheeses, salt, and pepper and mix well.

3. Serve right away or transfer to an airtight container and refrigerate for up to 3 days.

Allen's Tip: **If you've ever considered purchasing a potato ricer, now is the time. The tool helps incorporate air into mashed potatoes to prevent gumminess and give them a lighter texture.**

White Sweet Potato Biscuits

Biscuits are one of my favorite baked goods, and I know I'm not alone there. My wife and I enjoy noshing on these warm goodies spread with a little European butter while watching our favorite TV shows and sipping Earl Grey tea. In this recipe, I have incorporated white sweet potatoes, which are a touch less sweet and work well in a biscuit because they have a lower moisture content than other sweet potatoes.

MAKES 12–14 BISCUITS

3 medium white sweet potatoes (1 pound)
2 cups all-purpose flour
2 teaspoons baking soda
1 teaspoon baking powder
½ teaspoon kosher salt

6 tablespoons unsalted butter, cut into 12 pieces, at room temperature
½–1 cup buttermilk, plus more for brushing
European butter, strawberry jam, or honey, for serving (optional)

1. Preheat the oven to 400°F.

2. Put the potatoes on a rimmed baking sheet and bake for 35 to 40 minutes, until a sharp knife easily pierces the potatoes. Halve the potatoes lengthwise. Using a potholder, hold each half over a bowl and scoop the flesh from the potatoes into the bowl. Discard the peels. Using a potato masher, mash the potatoes until smooth. Refrigerate, covered, for at least 30 minutes or up to 24 hours.

3. In a large bowl, whisk together the flour, baking soda, baking powder, and salt. Add the butter and, using a pastry blender or two knives, cut it into the flour until the butter is incorporated and the mixture has a coarse, crumb-like texture.

4. Whisk the chilled sweet potato to ensure that it's smooth. Add it to the flour mixture, mixing well. Add ½ cup of the buttermilk and stir. The dough should be slightly sticky. If it seems dry, add up to ½ cup more of the buttermilk, 1 tablespoon at a time. Knead the mixture with your hands in the bowl two or three times until the dough just comes together.

5. Turn out the dough onto a floured work surface and pat to flatten it out to ½-inch thickness. Using a 2½-inch round biscuit cutter, cut out the biscuits. Transfer them to an ungreased rimmed baking sheet. Reroll the dough scraps and cut them again.

6. Brush the tops of the biscuits with buttermilk. Bake for about 15 minutes, or until the biscuits are browned and well risen.

7. Serve hot with butter, jam, or honey, if desired.

Creamy Twice-Baked Potatoes

My father's favorite side dish to make when I was growing up was twice-baked potatoes, often served as part of a steak dinner or alongside other meat mains. In this version, I've added cream cheese for a creamier, smoother texture.

SERVES 2

2 large russet potatoes

2 tablespoons unsalted butter, at room temperature

1 tablespoon whole milk

Salt and freshly ground black pepper, to taste

1 (3-ounce) package cream cheese, cubed

2 tablespoons sour cream

Paprika, for garnish

2 tablespoons chopped fresh chives, for garnish (optional)

1. Preheat the oven to 450°F.

2. Using a fork, prick each potato several times. Place the potatoes on a rimmed baking sheet and bake for about 1 hour, or until a sharp knife easily pierces the potatoes. Remove the potatoes from the oven and set aside to cool for 15 minutes. Reduce the oven temperature to 350°F.

3. Cut a thin slice lengthwise off each potato. Scoop out the flesh, leaving a ¼-inch-thick shell, and transfer the flesh to a medium bowl. Add the butter, milk, salt, and pepper. Using a handheld electric mixer, beat the potato mixture until smooth and fluffy. Add the cream cheese and sour cream and mix by hand until combined. Taste and add salt and pepper as needed.

4. Spoon the mixture evenly into the potato shells and return to the baking sheet. Sprinkle paprika over the potatoes.

5. Bake until the potatoes are heated through and the tops are golden brown, 20 to 25 minutes. Garnish with the chives, if desired, and serve right away.

Baby Red, Blue, and Purple Potatoes with Crème Fraîche and Chives

This simple yet colorful dish brightens up any dinner or lunch and makes for a beautiful presentation. I came up with the idea for this recipe after coming across a pasta dish incorporating crème fraîche and figured potatoes might hold up even better. Baby red, blue, and purple potatoes have a low starch content with a creamy, firm flesh that maintains its shape after cooking.

SERVES 4–6

7–9 baby Red Bliss or heirloom red potatoes (1 pound)

9–11 medium blue and purple potatoes (1½ pounds)

Sea salt and freshly ground black pepper, to taste

⅓ cup crème fraîche

2 tablespoons extra virgin olive oil

1 cup chopped fresh chives, for garnish

Grated Parmesan or Pecorino Romano, for garnish (optional)

1. Put the potatoes in a large saucepan and add enough cold salted water to cover them by 2 inches. Bring to a boil over high heat. Reduce the heat to medium and simmer for about 15 minutes, or until a sharp knife easily pierces the potatoes. Drain the potatoes in a colander and rinse them with cold water to cool.

2. When the potatoes are cool enough to handle, peel the potatoes and cut lengthwise into ¼-inch-thick slices. Season with salt and pepper. In a large skillet, combine the crème fraîche and potatoes and warm over medium heat until just heated through, 1 to 2 minutes.

3. Spoon the potato mixture onto serving plates. Drizzle with the olive oil and garnish with the chives and cheese, if desired. Serve right away.

Scalloped Potato and Clam Gratin

One day, while making a classic clam chowder and a potato gratin, it occurred to me that these two dishes would taste great combined. So I married the two in a casserole and voilà! My instincts were correct. That's the beauty of the versatile potato—it goes with everything.

SERVES 2

1 small russet potato, peeled and rinsed
1 tablespoon extra virgin olive oil
2 cloves garlic, minced
⅓ cup canned white clam sauce

Juice of ½ lemon
3 tablespoons grated Parmesan, divided
1 teaspoon poppy seeds
Chopped fresh basil, for garnish

1. Preheat the oven to 400°F.

2. Using a mandoline or very sharp knife, cut the potato crosswise into ½-inch-thick slices. Put the potato slices in a large saucepan and add enough cold salted water to cover them by 2 inches. Bring to a gentle boil over medium heat and simmer for 3 minutes, or until the potato slices have softened. Drain them in a colander and set aside.

3. Meanwhile, in an 8- to 10-inch sauté pan, heat the oil over medium heat until it shimmers. Add the garlic and sauté for 2 to 3 minutes. Add the clam sauce and simmer for 3 minutes, or until heated through. Stir in the lemon juice and 1½ tablespoons of the Parmesan. Using tongs, carefully add the potato slices to the clam sauce mixture and stir to cover all the slices.

4. Remove the sauté pan from the heat and use the tongs to arrange the potato slices (with liquid clinging to them) in a 6-inch circle on a rimmed baking sheet. Add three more layers of the potato slices in the same fashion, creating an overlapping circle that is 4 potato slices tall. Sprinkle the remaining 1½ tablespoons of Parmesan and the poppy seeds over the potato slices.

5. Bake for 7 to 10 minutes, until the top layer is golden brown. Remove from the oven, garnish with basil, and serve.

Crispy Potato Galettes

This is a quick and easy dish that works as a breakfast, brunch, or dinner side. I love the contrast between the outer crispy edges and soft, au gratin–like interior. You'll find these galettes used in my recipe for French Onion Soup (page 75) as a sturdier, more flavorful replacement for the baguette slice. Consider making extra or saving the leftovers for that recipe, too!

MAKES 2 (10- TO 12-INCH) CAKES

9 tablespoons olive oil, divided, plus more if needed
1 tablespoon fine sea salt
1 tablespoon freshly ground black pepper
2 teaspoons granulated garlic
2 teaspoons dried rosemary, crushed
1 teaspoon ground mustard
1 teaspoon ground nutmeg
2 medium russet potatoes, peeled and rinsed
4 tablespoons shredded Asiago
Chopped fresh chives, for garnish
1 recipe Zesty Sour Cream (page 177) or plain sour cream, for serving

1. In a small bowl, combine 3 tablespoons of the olive oil with the salt, pepper, garlic, rosemary, mustard, and nutmeg. Mix well with a pastry brush and set aside. Using a mandoline or sharp knife, cut the potatoes crosswise into ⅛-inch-thick slices. Set half of the potato slices aside.

2. Pour another 3 tablespoons of the olive oil into a 10- to 12-inch cast iron or heavy-bottomed skillet. Place 1 potato slice in the center and, working from the center out, arrange the other slices overlapping each other in an attractive spiral layer. Using a pastry brush, gently brush a thin layer of the oil-spice mixture over the potato layer, being careful not to shift the potatoes. Sprinkle 1 tablespoon of the Asiago over the layer. In the same fashion, add a second layer of the potatoes, brush it with the oil-spice mixture, and sprinkle with another 1 tablespoon of the Asiago. Repeat this process a third time but do not add the cheese to the top layer.

3. Place the skillet over medium-high heat. Using a wide, flat spatula, gently press down so the potatoes start to stick to each other. Cook for 10 to 12 minutes, until the bottom is starting to brown and crisp. Using the spatula, very gently flip the potatoes, which by now should be a solid cake, to the raw side and continue cooking for another 10 minutes, or until the potatoes are golden brown on both sides and a sharp knife easily pierces the potatoes. Add additional olive oil if the skillet starts to smoke and dry. If the potatoes are browning too quickly, reduce the heat. Slide the potato cake out of the skillet and onto a plate.

4. Repeat this process with the reserved half of the potato slices and the remaining oil-spice mixture and Asiago to make another cake, and fry it in the remaining 3 tablespoons of olive oil in the same manner.

5. To serve, cut the cakes into wedges and transfer to a plate or platter. Garnish with chives and serve, with sour cream on the side, if desired.

Allen's Tip: **To make 4 (6-inch) cakes for the French Onion Soup (page 75), cook 2 of the cakes at a time in the same skillet.**

Potato Stuffing Casserole

I enjoy all dishes on Thanksgiving, but I was never a huge fan of the apple stuffing my parents made while I was growing up. Instead, I created a similar, but more savory, version using potatoes that my family has come to love. If you do happen to make this for Thanksgiving, try topping off the casserole with a little turkey gravy for some extra indulgence.

SERVES 6–8

4–5 large russet potatoes, peeled and
    rinsed
4 tablespoons unsalted butter, divided
2 celery ribs, chopped (about ¼ cup)
1 medium yellow onion, chopped
1 (7-inch) baguette, cut into ¾-inch cubes
¼ cup chopped fresh flat-leaf parsley, plus
    more for garnish

1 tablespoon salt
½ teaspoon freshly ground black pepper
1 cup light cream, hot
1 large egg, beaten
¼ cup grated Parmesan

1. Preheat the oven to 350°F. Grease a shallow 1½-quart baking dish.

2. Put the potatoes in a large saucepan and add enough cold salted water to cover them by 2 inches. Bring to a boil over high heat. Reduce the heat to medium and simmer for about 15 minutes, or until a sharp knife easily pierces the potatoes. Drain the potatoes and return them to the saucepan off the heat. Using a potato masher, mash the potatoes while they are still hot. Set them aside.

3. In a medium skillet, melt 2 tablespoons of the butter over medium heat until the foaming subsides. Add the celery and onion and sauté until tender. Add the bread and cook, stirring, until lightly browned. Stir in the mashed potatoes, parsley, salt, pepper, cream, and egg and mix well.

4. Spoon the potato mixture into the prepared baking dish. Dot with small pieces of the remaining 2 tablespoons of butter. Bake for 30 to 40 minutes, until the casserole is lightly browned and bubbly. During the last 10 minutes of baking, sprinkle the Parmesan over the top.

5. Garnish with parsley and serve.

Slow-Roasted Root Vegetable and Potato Purée

Fall on the East Coast for me signals the time for root vegetables like turnips, parsnips, and sweet potatoes. Instead of a straight potato purée, this multidimensional blend has an earthy, rich taste, making it the perfect base for all types of proteins, from braised beef or oxtail to pork chops, fried chicken, and even meaty fish.

SERVES 4

3 medium russet potatoes, peeled, rinsed, and cut into 1-inch cubes

2 medium sweet potatoes, peeled, rinsed, and cut into 1-inch cubes

2 parsnips, peeled and cut into 1-inch cubes

2 turnips, peeled and cut into 1-inch cubes

1 medium yellow onion, cut into 1-inch chunks

4 cloves garlic, peeled

3 tablespoons olive oil

2 teaspoons salt, plus more to taste

2 teaspoons freshly ground black pepper, plus more to taste

1 cup heavy cream, plus more as needed

3 tablespoons unsalted butter, at room temperature

1. Preheat the oven to 250°F.

2. In a large bowl, toss together the potatoes, sweet potatoes, parsnips, turnips, onion, garlic, olive oil, salt, and pepper. Transfer to a large casserole dish. Bake, stirring and tossing halfway through, for 3 hours, or until the vegetables are tender.

3. Spoon the vegetables (in batches, if necessary) into the bowl of a food processor. Add the cream and butter and purée until the mixture is smooth. Taste and add salt and pepper as needed.

4. If necessary, reheat the purée by transferring it to a saucepan set over medium heat and whisking until it is heated through and smooth. If needed, add a bit of heavy cream to loosen it. Transfer the purée to a serving bowl and serve hot.

Sweet Buttered Steak Fries

These classic thick-cut fries are the perfect pairing for burgers or steaks, but they also make for great edible "utensils" on their own when dipped in a variety of condiments and sauces. I find that pan-frying the potatoes in butter makes for a tastier, easier preparation versus the mess of deep-frying them in oil. The butter also adds a slight sweetness. Feel free to double, triple, or even quadruple the recipe for a crowd.

SERVES 2

1 medium russet potato, peeled and rinsed
2 tablespoons unsalted butter
Kosher salt, to taste

1. Halve the potato lengthwise and then cut each half lengthwise into ½-inch-thick strips.

2. In a large sauté pan, melt the butter over medium heat until the foaming subsides. Add the potato and cook, spooning the butter over the fries and turning them once, for about 10 minutes, or until golden brown on all sides.

3. Transfer to a serving dish and season with salt. Serve right away.

Ultimate Blue Cheese Potato Gratin

Blue cheese holds a special place in my heart for its unique, robust flavor. But I know that not everyone loves this pungent delicacy as much as I do. For those of you on that side of the fence, this recipe just might change your mind. There's just enough blue cheese but not so much that it overpowers the whole dish, and the árbol chiles spice things up a bit. I prefer a smoked blue cheese, which has less pungency and more earthiness than traditional blue cheese.

SERVES 8–10

2 large russet potatoes
3 slices thick-cut bacon
1 cup whole milk
¾ cup heavy cream
1 small yellow onion, chopped
3 dried chiles de árbol (optional)
½ teaspoon chili powder
½ teaspoon salt, plus more to taste

½ teaspoon freshly ground black pepper, plus more to taste
2 tablespoons unsalted butter
2 tablespoons all-purpose flour
¾ cup shredded Gruyère
1 cup crumbled blue cheese or smoked blue cheese, divided
Sliced scallions, for garnish

1. Preheat the oven to 375°F. Grease the bottom of a 12-inch oval or an 8-inch square baking dish.

2. Using a mandoline or very sharp knife, cut the potatoes crosswise into ⅛-inch-thick rounds and transfer them to a bowl of cold water. Drain well in a colander and rinse the potatoes with cold water. Let stand in the colander to dry.

3. Place the bacon slices on a rimmed baking sheet and bake for about 10 minutes, or until crisp. Transfer to paper towels to drain and set aside. When cool enough to handle, chop or crumble into small bits.

4. Meanwhile, in a small saucepan, combine the milk, cream, onion, chiles (if using), chili powder, salt, and pepper. Bring to a simmer over low heat and cook, whisking occasionally, for 5 minutes. Strain the sauce mixture through a fine-mesh strainer into a bowl and discard the contents of the strainer.

5. In the same saucepan, melt the butter over medium heat until the foaming subsides. Add the flour and whisk until combined. Cook, whisking vigorously to remove lumps, for 1 minute. Add the sauce mixture, Gruyère, and ½ cup of the blue cheese, stirring until the cheese is melted.

6. Arrange a third of the potatoes in the prepared baking dish in an overlapping layer. Season with salt and pepper and add a third of the cheese sauce, using a rubber spatula to spread it. Repeat this process until all the potatoes are gone, making sure the last layer of potatoes is topped with the cheese sauce.

7. Bake for 45 minutes, or until the potatoes are tender. Remove the dish from the oven and crumble the remaining ½ cup of blue cheese over the top. Return the dish to the oven just long enough to melt the cheese, 3 to 5 minutes.

8. Remove the dish from the oven and let stand for 5 minutes. Garnish with the bacon crumbles and scallions and serve.

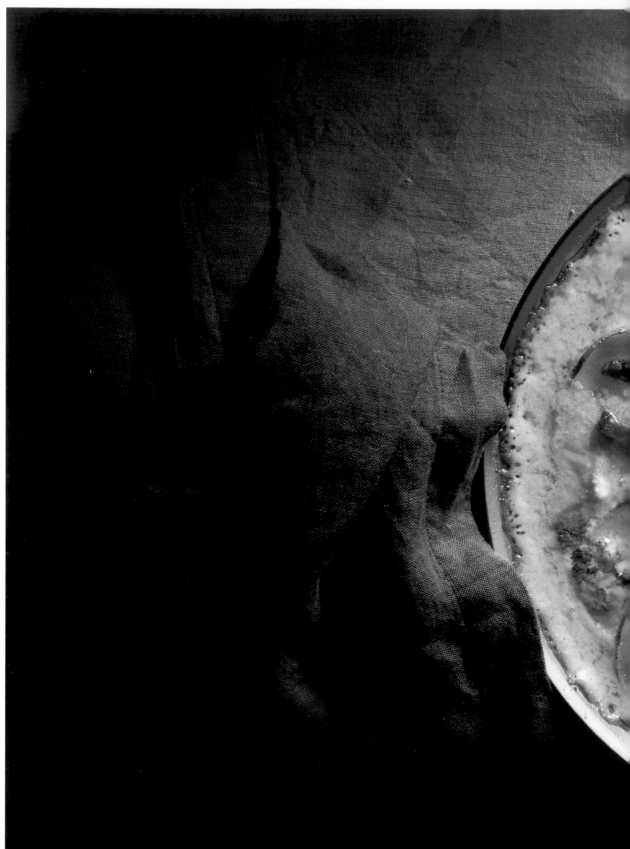

Ultimate Blue Cheese Potato Gratin (p.153)

CHAPTER 6:
Sweets

Potatoes in a dessert? Sure, sweet potatoes make sense, but believe it or not, traditional white and russet potatoes can taste just as delicious when made into an end-of-the-meal sweet or occasional treat.

Black and White Chocolate-Covered Potato Chips

Are you as big a fan of salted caramel as I am? The combination of sweet and salty can't be beat. Serve this treat at parties and it'll be a "once you pop, you can't stop" situation.

SERVES 2–4

1 cup semisweet chocolate chips
2 tablespoons vegetable shortening, divided
1 cup white chocolate chips
1 recipe Homemade Thick-Cut Potato Chips (page 172),
    or 1 (6½-ounce) bag favorite plain potato chips

1. Line a rimmed baking sheet with wax paper and set it aside.

2. In a small microwave-safe bowl, combine the semisweet chocolate chips and 1 table-spoon of the shortening. In a separate microwave-safe dish, combine the white chocolate and remaining 1 tablespoon of shortening. Heat each dish, one at a time, in a microwave oven on medium power in 1-minute increments, stirring until melted and smooth. (Alternatively, melt each chocolate separately in a double boiler set over simmering water, stirring until melted.)

3. Dip the chips, one at a time, into the semisweet chocolate, coating half of each chip. Drag the chip against the edge of the dish to remove excess chocolate or use a spatula. Place all the chips on the prepared baking sheet and let stand until they are cool enough to handle and the chocolate is set.

4. Dip the other half of the chips, one at a time, into the white chocolate and return them to the baking sheet. Let stand at room temperature for 15 minutes. Transfer the baking sheet to the refrigerator and chill until they are completely set, at least 1 hour.

5. Transfer any leftovers to an airtight container and refrigerate for up to 1 week.

The Potatopia Cookbook

Mashed Potato Chocolate Truffles

Chocolate truffles are always a treat. One day, with some extra mashed potatoes in the fridge, I thought to add them to a traditional truffle recipe instead of the cream. Turns out potatoes make for a great—and healthier—substitute. Try this recipe whenever you end up with leftover mashed potatoes!

MAKES ABOUT 12 TRUFFLES

1 cup semisweet and/or dark chocolate
    chips
½ cup leftover plain mashed potatoes, cold
½ teaspoon pure vanilla extract

½ cup toppings for rolling, such as coconut
    flakes, powdered sugar, or finely
    chopped hazelnuts

1. Put the chocolate chips in a small microwave-safe bowl. Heat the chocolate in a microwave oven on medium power in 1-minute increments, stirring until melted and smooth. (Alternatively, melt the chocolate in a double boiler set over simmering water, stirring until melted.) Add the mashed potatoes and vanilla, stirring until fully blended. Transfer the mixture to the refrigerator to firm up for 30 minutes.

2. To shape the truffles, spoon out 1 tablespoon of the chocolate mixture and roll it into a ball between the palms of your hands. Roll the ball in your choice of topping, then place it on a plate. Repeat this process with the remaining chocolate mixture. Cover and refrigerate the truffles until firm, about 30 minutes.

3. Leftover truffles will keep in the refrigerator for about 1 week or in the freezer for up to 2 months.

Sweet Potato Blondies with Vanilla Ice Cream and Hazelnuts

One of my favorite desserts is blondies with coffee ice cream. Figuring that sweet potatoes could stand in for some of the butter and sugar in blondies, I came up with this recipe. Now I always use sweet potatoes in my blondies because of the extra flavor, moisture, and texture dimension they add. Pair these addictive treats with nutty hazelnuts and rich vanilla ice cream for an elegant plated dessert.

SERVES 8–10

1¼ cups sweet potato purée (see Allen's Tip)
¾ cup canola oil
¾ cup firmly packed brown sugar
⅓ cup granulated sugar
⅓ cup hazelnut-flavored nondairy creamer
  or half-and-half
1½ tablespoons ground flax seed
1½ teaspoons pure vanilla extract

2 cups unbleached all-purpose flour
1½ teaspoons baking powder
1½ teaspoons ground cinnamon
1 teaspoon ground nutmeg
½ teaspoon salt
Vanilla ice cream, for serving
¼ cup toasted hazelnuts, finely chopped or
  coarsely processed in a food processor

1. Preheat the oven to 350°F. Grease an 8-inch square baking dish or a 12-inch round or oval casserole dish.

2. In a medium bowl, whisk together the sweet potato purée, oil, brown sugar, granulated sugar, creamer, flax seed, and vanilla. Whisk until smooth.

3. In a small bowl, whisk together the flour, baking powder, cinnamon, nutmeg, and salt. Slowly mix the flour mixture into the sweet potato mixture until a thick batter forms; do not overmix.

4. Pour the batter into the prepared baking dish and smooth the top. Bake for 40 to 50 minutes, until golden brown and a toothpick inserted into the center comes out clean.

5. Remove from the oven and let the blondies cool completely. Cut into 8 or 10 bars and transfer to plates. Top each with a scoop of ice cream. Scatter the hazelnuts over the ice cream and serve.

Allen's Tip: **You can find canned sweet potato purée at the grocery store, but it's easy to make at home. To make the amount called for in this recipe, peel and rinse 1 large sweet potato. Cut it into 3-inch cubes and put them in a saucepan. Add enough cold water to cover the cubes by 2 inches. Bring to a boil over high heat. Reduce the heat to medium and cook for 20 to 30 minutes, until a sharp knife easily pierces the sweet potato cubes. Then drain them and mash until smooth. Let the purée cool for 30 minutes before using it in this recipe.**

Sweet Potato Pound Cake

My wife Galina's favorite dessert—hands down—is pound cake with milk or tea. But when I told her I would try a potato version, she wasn't exactly thrilled. Turns out, she loved the lightened-up version and now requests it at least once a month! Try a slice topped with ice cream or whipped cream.

SERVES 12

Pound Cake
1 cup (2 sticks) unsalted butter, at room temperature
2 cups granulated sugar
4 large eggs
1 teaspoon pure vanilla extract
3 cups all-purpose flour
2 teaspoons baking powder
1 teaspoon ground cinnamon
½ teaspoon baking soda

¼ teaspoon salt
¼ teaspoon ground nutmeg
2 cups sweet potato purée (see Allen's Tip, page 160), cold

Glaze
1 tablespoon unsalted butter
¼ cup powdered sugar
2 tablespoons 2 percent milk
½ teaspoon pure vanilla extract

1. Preheat the oven to 350°F. Grease and flour a 10-inch tube pan.

2. **For the pound cake:** In a large bowl, beat the butter and sugar until light and fluffy. Add the eggs, one at a time, beating well after each addition. Stir in the vanilla. In a separate bowl, whisk together the flour, baking powder, cinnamon, baking soda, salt, and nutmeg. Add the flour mixture to the egg mixture and mix just until the dry ingredients are moistened. Stir in the sweet potato purée just until combined.

3. Pour the batter into the prepared pan. Bake for 50 to 60 minutes, until a toothpick inserted near the center of the cake comes out clean. Cool for 10 minutes, then remove the cake from the pan and transfer it to a wire rack to cool completely.

4. **For the glaze:** In a small skillet, melt the butter over medium heat and cook for 2 minutes, or until lightly browned. Remove from the heat. Whisk in the sugar, milk, and vanilla until smooth.

5. Drizzle the warm glaze over the cake. Wait at least 1 hour for the glaze to harden, then slice and serve.

Sweet Potato Cobbler

My business partners Alex and Dimitry both love apple cobbler and often order it when it's on the menu at restaurants. They always offer to share, but I'm just not a fan of cooked apples. But then it occurred to me to swap out the apples for smooth sweet potatoes. Success! Make it even more memorable with a little ice cream on top.

SERVES 6-8

8 tablespoons (1 stick) plus ⅓ cup unsalted butter, divided
3 tablespoons whipping cream
¾ cup granulated sugar
½ cup firmly packed brown sugar
1¼ teaspoons ground cinnamon

¼ teaspoon salt
1 large sweet potato, peeled, rinsed, and thinly sliced (1½ pounds)
1⅔ cups self-rising flour
½ cup buttermilk, plus more as needed

1. Preheat the oven to 350°F.

2. In a 10-inch cast iron or oven-safe skillet, melt 8 tablespoons of the butter over medium heat until the foaming subsides. Whisk in the whipping cream, granulated sugar, brown sugar, cinnamon, and salt. Remove from the heat.

3. Layer the sweet potato slices evenly in the mixture. Cover the skillet with aluminum foil, place on a rimmed baking sheet, and transfer it to the oven. Bake for 25 minutes, or until a sharp knife easily pierces the sweet potato slices.

4. In a medium bowl, using a pastry blender or two knives, cut the remaining ⅓ cup of butter into the flour until crumbly. Stir in the buttermilk just until the dry ingredients are moistened. If more moisture is needed, add more buttermilk, 1 teaspoon at a time.

5. Turn out the dough onto a lightly floured work surface and knead it three or four times. Pat or roll the dough into a 10-inch circle. Place the dough evenly over the cobbler.

6. Bake, uncovered, for 25 minutes, or until golden brown. Cut into wedges and serve warm.

APPENDIX A:
Basic Potato Recipes

Creamy Mashed Potatoes

SERVES 8–10

12–13 medium Yukon Gold potatoes,
    quartered (3½ pounds)
1 tablespoon olive oil
6 tablespoons unsalted butter, cubed

1½ cups light cream or half-and-half, plus
    more as needed
1 cup mascarpone cheese
Salt and freshly ground black pepper, to taste

1. Put the potatoes in a large saucepan and add enough cold salted water to cover them by 2 inches. Add the olive oil and bring to a boil over medium-high heat. Reduce the heat to medium and simmer for about 15 minutes, or until a sharp knife easily pierces the potatoes. Drain the potatoes and return them to the hot pan.

2. Add the butter and cream and, using a potato masher, mash the mixture until it is smooth with absolutely no chunks. Add the mascarpone and continue mixing with the potato masher. Season with salt and pepper. For a smoother texture, transfer the potatoes to the bowl of a food processor and pulse until smooth and creamy. Add more cream if the mixture is not smooth enough.

3. If the potatoes have cooled, simply reheat them, stirring often, over medium heat with a little extra cream, until heated through.

Allen's Tip: When I use these potatoes for recipes such as my "Everything Bagel" Potato Croquettes (page 43) or Mashed Potato Bacon Bites (page 42), I usually chill them for up to 24 hours. Not only does this allow me to organize my prep time, but the refrigerator's cold temperature stiffens the texture of the mashed potatoes so that they are easier to work with. Be sure to cover the bowl holding the potatoes with a lid or plastic wrap.

Golden Potato Chips

MAKES ABOUT 50 CHIPS

5 baby Yukon Gold potatoes
3 cups rice bran or other neutral vegetable oil

1. Using a mandoline or very sharp knife and working over a bowl of cold water, cut the potatoes into ⅛-inch-thick slices, letting them fall into the water. Drain the potato slices, blot them with paper towels, and transfer them to a rimmed baking sheet to dry completely.

2. In a medium saucepan, heat the oil over high heat until it shimmers and a deep-fry thermometer registers 375°F.

3. Working in batches so as not to crowd the pan, add a handful of the potato slices and fry for 1 minute, or until golden brown. Stir the potatoes with tongs to prevent them from sticking together. Using a slotted spoon, transfer the potatoes to paper towels to drain. Allow the oil to regain temperature between batches.

Allen's Tip: To make extra-crispy chips, use a blow-dryer before you fry them. Yep, that's right. You have to dry the chips very well before frying or they won't get as crispy. Instead of using paper towels to blot the chips, place them on a rimmed baking sheet and hold a blow-dryer 8 to 9 inches away from the chips, moving over them to dry out the water for 3 to 5 minutes. (It's tempting to just put the whole tray in the oven instead, but doing so may cause the chips to steam.)

Jersey Sweet Potato Chips

MAKES 20-25 CHIPS

1 large sweet potato (preferably Jersey), peeled and rinsed
2 cups rice bran or other neutral vegetable oil
Sea salt, for sprinkling

1. Using a mandoline or sharp knife, cut the potato crosswise into ⅛-inch-thick slices. Immediately after cutting, submerge the potato slices in a large bowl of cold water to prevent browning.

2. Drain the potato slices and gently blot with a clean kitchen towel. Spread the slices on another kitchen towel to dry completely. The potato slices should be as dry as possible.

3. In a deep 12-inch skillet, heat the oil over medium-high heat until it shimmers and a deep-fry thermometer registers 350°F.

4. Working in batches so as not to crowd the pan, add 2 potato slices and set a smaller heavy skillet on top of them, taking care that it does not cause the oil to overflow. This will ensure that the potato slices are as flat as possible and do not curl during frying. Fry for about 3 minutes, or until golden brown. Using a slotted spoon, transfer the chips to paper towels to drain, and season with salt while hot. Allow the oil to regain temperature between batches.

The Potatopia Cookbook

Shoestring Fries

SERVES 2-4

2 medium white or russet potatoes
3 cups rice bran or other neutral vegetable oil
Kosher salt, to taste

1. Using a mandoline or very sharp knife, cut the potatoes lengthwise into ⅛-inch-thick slices. Stack the slices and carefully cut them lengthwise again into ¼-inch-thick strips. Soak the shoestrings in a bowl of cold water for a few minutes and then pat them dry with paper towels.

2. In a large, deep saucepan, heat the oil over medium heat until it shimmers and a deep-fry thermometer registers 375°F.

3. Working in batches so as not to crowd the pan, add a handful of the potatoes and fry for 2 to 3 minutes, until golden brown. Stir the potatoes with tongs to prevent them from sticking together. Using a slotted spoon, transfer the potatoes to paper towels to drain, and season with salt while still hot. Allow the oil to regain temperature between batches.

Potato Gnocchi

SERVES 4–6

3 medium russet potatoes
1 tablespoon salt
¼ cup grated Parmesan
1 cup all-purpose flour, plus more for rolling
1 large egg, lightly beaten

1. Preheat the oven to 375°F.

2. Using a fork, prick each potato several times. Place them on a rimmed baking sheet and bake for about 1 hour, or until the potatoes are tender all the way through. Remove them from the oven and set aside until cool enough to handle.

3. Peel the potatoes and run them through a potato ricer or box grater back onto the baking sheet. Refrigerate the riced potatoes until they are cold, about 30 minutes.

4. Put the riced potatoes in a mound on a floured working surface. Sprinkle the salt, Parmesan, and flour over the potatoes. Create a well in the center of the potatoes and add the beaten egg. Begin mixing the ingredients together with your hands and lightly kneading the dough until it just comes together without separating. If the dough is too sticky, add more flour, but be careful not to add too much or to over-knead, as this will make the gnocchi heavy and tough.

5. Shape the dough into several long ropes that are about ½ inch in diameter. Cut each rope into ¾-inch pieces. With a floured finger, make a dimple in each dough ball as you press it gently against a floured fork. Transfer the gnocchi to a lightly floured surface and keep them from touching each other. Use immediately for Potato Gnocchi Carbonara with Pancetta (page 108) or Pan-Fried Potato Gnocchi with Spinach (page 135), or freeze for up to 3 months (see Allen's Tip).

Allen's Tip: **The best way to freeze gnocchi is to first lay them out on a rimmed baking sheet in a single layer and pop that in the freezer. Once the gnocchi are frozen solid, transfer them to a zip-top bag to save space in the freezer. Be sure to fully thaw the gnocchi (overnight in the refrigerator) before cooking them; otherwise the outsides can disintegrate in the boiling water before the middles are cooked through.**

The Potatopia Cookbook

Homemade Thick-Cut Potato Chips

MAKES 8–10 CHIPS

2 medium russet potatoes
3 tablespoons olive oil or herb-flavored olive oil, such as basil
1 teaspoon coarse sea salt
1 teaspoon freshly ground black pepper

1. Preheat the oven to 375°F. Grease a rimmed baking sheet and set it aside.

2. Cut the potatoes lengthwise into ½-inch-thick slices. In a small bowl, combine the olive oil, salt, and pepper. Place the potatoes in a single layer on the prepared baking sheet and brush both sides of the potato slices with the oil mixture.

3. Bake the potato slices for 6 minutes. Flip the slices and continue to bake for 7 to 8 minutes, until the potatoes are tender and the edges are browned. Serve right away.

APPENDIX B:
The Sauces

Ranch Dip

MAKES ABOUT 2¼ CUPS

1 cup sour cream
1 cup mayonnaise
2 teaspoons minced fresh garlic
2 teaspoons minced yellow onion
2 teaspoons chopped fresh flat-leaf parsley

2 teaspoons chopped fresh dill
1 teaspoon salt
1 teaspoon freshly ground white pepper
1 teaspoon granulated sugar

Combine all the ingredients in a serving bowl and mix well. Transfer to an airtight container and refrigerate for at least 1 hour or up to 2 days.

Spicy Sesame Aioli

MAKES ABOUT 1 CUP

½ cup mayonnaise
¼ cup sour cream
Juice of ½ lemon
1 tablespoon spicy brown mustard
¾ teaspoon toasted sesame oil

¾ teaspoon distilled white vinegar
2 tablespoons chopped fresh dill
½ teaspoon cayenne pepper
⅛ teaspoon sea salt
⅛ teaspoon freshly ground black pepper

Combine all the ingredients in a food processor and process until smooth. Transfer to an airtight container and refrigerate for at least 1 hour or up to 1 day.

Hollandaise Sauce

MAKES ABOUT ¾ CUP

6 tablespoons unsalted butter
4 large egg yolks
1 tablespoon freshly squeezed lemon juice

1 teaspoon salt
1 teaspoon freshly ground black pepper

1. In a small saucepan, slowly melt the butter over medium-low heat. Do not let it boil.

2. Fill a medium saucepan halfway with water and bring to a simmer over medium-low heat. Combine the egg yolks and lemon juice in a heat-safe bowl and place the bowl over the saucepan. While whisking the yolks vigorously, add the hot butter in a stream until the sauce thickens.

3. Whisk in the salt and pepper. Place near the stovetop until ready to use or for up to 1 hour; this will keep it warm but not cause it to thicken too much. If it starts to thicken, whisk in 1 to 2 tablespoons of warm water to thin it. Serve immediately or transfer to an airtight container within 2 hours of cooking and refrigerate for up to 3 days.

Allen's Tip: **Instead of whisking, you can use a blender. Blend the yolks, lemon juice, salt, and pepper until well combined. Remove the cap from the center of the blender lid and, while the machine is running, add the hot butter in a stream until the sauce thickens. Transfer it to a saucepan and heat before serving.**

Hot Ginger Sauce

MAKES ABOUT 2½ CUPS

1 cup rice vinegar
1 cup water
½ cup granulated sugar
2 tablespoons ketchup

2 teaspoons seeded and chopped serrano
   chile
2 teaspoons minced fresh ginger
1 teaspoon minced garlic
2 teaspoons cornstarch (optional)

In the bowl of a food processor, combine the vinegar, water, sugar, ketchup, chile, ginger, and garlic. Pulse a few times to mix well. If you prefer a thicker sauce, add the cornstarch and pulse to mix. Serve immediately or refrigerate in an airtight container for up to 2 days.

Creamy Kimchi Dip

MAKES ABOUT 2 CUPS

1 cup mayonnaise
1½ cups hot kimchi
1 tablespoon wasabi mayonnaise

1½ teaspoons rice vinegar
1½ teaspoons soy sauce

Combine all the ingredients in the bowl of a food processor and process until well blended. Transfer to an airtight container and refrigerate for at least 1 hour or up to 2 weeks.

Béchamel Sauce

MAKES ABOUT 2½ CUPS

2 cups whole milk
2 teaspoons whole black peppercorns
2 bay leaves
1 cinnamon stick
½ medium yellow onion, chopped

2 tablespoons unsalted butter
2 tablespoons all-purpose flour
½ cup grated Gruyère
Kosher salt, to taste

1. In a large saucepan, heat the milk over medium heat for about 1 minute; do not let it boil. Stir in the peppercorns, bay leaves, cinnamon stick, and onion. Cook, whisking frequently, for 5 to 7 minutes, until the milk foams up; do not let it boil. Strain the milk mixture and discard the contents of the strainer.

2. Wipe out the saucepan. Melt the butter in the pan over medium heat until the foaming subsides. Add the flour and cook, stirring constantly with a wooden spoon, for about 2 minutes, or until a paste forms. While stirring constantly, add the strained milk. Then stir in the cheese and mix well. Taste and add salt as needed. Serve immediately or transfer to an airtight container and refrigerate for up to 2 hours.

3. To reheat the sauce, transfer it to a saucepan and heat over medium heat, whisking constantly, until it returns to a smooth sauce.

Russian Dressing

MAKES ABOUT 1½ CUPS

1 cup mayonnaise
¼ cup ketchup
4 teaspoons prepared horseradish
1 tablespoon minced yellow onion

1 teaspoon hot pepper sauce
1 teaspoon Worcestershire sauce
¼ teaspoon paprika

Combine all the ingredients in a small bowl and whisk well until combined. Transfer the dressing to an airtight container and refrigerate for at least 1 hour or up to 2 days.

Herbed Yogurt Dip

MAKES ABOUT ⅔ CUP

½ cup plain Greek-style yogurt
1½ tablespoons chopped fresh flat-leaf parsley
1½ teaspoons chopped fresh dill
1½ teaspoons chopped fresh chives
1½ teaspoons minced scallion, white and light green parts only

1½ teaspoons thinly sliced fresh basil
½ teaspoon red wine vinegar
½ teaspoon freshly squeezed lemon juice
Salt and freshly ground black pepper, to taste

Combine all the ingredients in a small bowl and mix well. Transfer to an airtight container and refrigerate for at least 1 hour or up to 3 weeks.

Tangy Pepper Sauce

MAKES ABOUT 2 CUPS

1½ cups mayonnaise
1 cup fresh flat-leaf parsley leaves
3 tablespoons olive oil
2 Padrón peppers, seeded, roasted, and peeled (see Allen's Tip)
3 anchovies in oil, drained
1 tablespoon white wine vinegar

1 tablespoon chopped fresh chives
1 tablespoon sour cream
2 teaspoons freshly squeezed lime juice
½ jalapeño, seeded if desired and chopped
Salt and freshly ground black pepper, to taste

Combine all the ingredients in the bowl of a food processor and process until fairly smooth. Taste and add salt and pepper if necessary. Transfer to an airtight container and refrigerate for at least 1 hour or up to 3 days.

Allen's Tip: **To quick-roast the peppers, slice them in half, remove the seeds, and broil them in the oven or toaster oven, turning occasionally, until blackened. Cover them with paper or kitchen towels for a few minutes to loosen the skin, then peel off the skins. It's okay if a little of the blackened skin remains; that will add to the smoky flavor.**

Tartar Sauce

MAKES ABOUT 1½ CUPS

1 cup mayonnaise
½ cup minced sweet pickles
2 tablespoons freshly squeezed lemon juice

Pinch salt
Pinch ground white pepper

Combine all the ingredients in a small bowl and mix well. Transfer to an airtight container and refrigerate for at least 1 hour or up to 2 days.

Allen's Pesto

MAKES ABOUT 1 CUP

2 cups packed fresh basil leaves
¼ cup pine nuts or toasted walnuts
2 cloves garlic, peeled

½ cup freshly grated Pecorino Romano or Parmesan
⅔ cup extra virgin olive oil
Freshly ground black pepper, to taste

1. Combine the basil and pine nuts in the bowl of a food processor and pulse until coarsely chopped. Add the garlic and cheese and pulse to combine.

2. With the machine running, add the oil in a steady stream through the feed tube, scraping down the bowl as needed, until emulsified. Season generously with black pepper. Serve immediately or transfer to an airtight container and refrigerate for up to 3 weeks.

Zesty Sour Cream

MAKES ABOUT 1 CUP

1 cup sour cream
1 small shallot, chopped

1 teaspoon cayenne pepper
½ teaspoon finely grated lime zest

Combine all the ingredients in a small bowl and mix well. Transfer to an airtight container and refrigerate for at least 1 hour or up to 2 days.

Acknowledgments

This book was a great undertaking, and I couldn't have done it without a number of important people.

Thank you, first and foremost, to Doug Seibold at Agate, who believed in my idea for a cookbook that would bring culinary attention back to the humble potato. I would also like to thank my agent, Karen Gantz, for believing in and helping to present my ideas.

Thank you to my dear parents, Mark and Anna Dikker, for raising me with great values and a strong work ethic. I am most grateful to you for the sense of freedom you instilled in me that, until this day, allows me to follow my dreams without hesitation.

A warm thanks to my brother and sister, Milan and Rolanda Dikker. Milan, my older brother and my best friend, you have always been there for me and you continue to be my sounding board to this day. Rolanda, my baby sister, you are one of my greatest supporters and a fellow food enthusiast, and your advice is always spot on.

Of course, a huge thank you goes to my beautiful wife, Galina Kotovets-Dikker. I knew I wanted to marry you from the minute I first saw you. You have been my rock and inspiration through multiple business ventures and in life, and you are a wonderful mom to our two amazing boys, Landen and Kyle, who together are the best taste testers and critics in the kitchen. More importantly, thank you, Galina, for telling me you would support the family in any way you could when I was even just contemplating launching Potatopia. I will always cherish you for the support and love you bring to our marriage and family.

There are a number of people in my Potatopia circle I would like to acknowledge for their enduring support, passion, and patience as I continued to expand my restaurant chain and—miraculously—work on this book at the same time. Thank you to my partners, Alex Fleyshmakher and Dimitry Meksin—your belief and patience in me is the glue that holds us together. I am truly blessed and honored to have you as partners and friends. Neither Potatopia nor this book would be here without your relentless support and dedication to the brand. To all my employees and franchisees, I thank you for your dedication to Potatopia and the hard work you show day in and day out. Thank you to Albert Sierra, my director of operations and friend. You have stuck by my side from the beginning, and I would not have been able to do it without you.

Thank you to Amelia Levin, my writer and collaborator who helped edit the recipes, write the book's content, and keep me on track throughout this entire process.

Thank you to the book's photographer, Melissa Hom; food stylist, Mira Evnine; and assistant food stylist, Shaw Lash, whose vision helped turn the text into beautiful and craveable imagery. Thank you Alan and Gilat Tunit for providing me with a beautiful kitchen that made the photo shoot perfect.

Also, a warm thanks to my restaurant designers, Fadi Riscala and Michelle Agnese. The day we met, you instantly believed in my crazy potato idea. Not only have you blessed me with innovative design and passion for the brand, but you also served as a sounding board when I needed one most.

And thanks to 5WPR, my public relations firm, as well as to Richard Kronengold and Kristen Cahill for their superior marketing and branding expertise. You helped shape the Potatopia brand from the very beginning.

Lastly, I would like to express gratitude to William Bulmer, another important key to the success of the Potatopia brand, and a great friend and mentor. Your advice in business and life has been paramount.

Thank you all so very much!

The Potatopia Cookbook

Index

About the Author

Allen Dikker is an entrepreneur who has successfully launched several businesses in industries such as real estate, media, and food. Most recently, he founded Potatopia, a fast-casual, all-potato concept restaurant that features high-quality ingredients and a range of signature sauces.

The Potatopia Cookbook